Christopher Gilchrist started his journalistic career on the *Financial Times*. He has written on investment and personal finance for many other newspapers and journals including *The Daily Telegraph*, *Daily Mail*, *The Sunday Times* and *Investors Chronicle*. He founded *What Investment* magazine and edited it for six years, and currently edits an investment newsletter, *The IRS Report*. He appears regularly on Radio 4's *MoneyBox* programme and other radio and TV programmes.

D1646171

Also available in this series:

The Sunday Times Personal Finance Guide to Your Pension
BY STEPHEN ELLIS

The Sunday Times Personal Finance Guide to the Protection Game
BY KEVIN PRATT

The Sunday Times Personal Finance Guide to Your Home
BY DIANA WRIGHT

The Sunday Times Personal Finance Guide to Your Retirement
BY DIANA WRIGHT

THE SUNDAY TIMES
Personal Finance Guide to

TAX-FREE SAVINGS

How to Make Your Money Work Hardest for You

Christopher Gilchrist

HarperCollins*Publishers*

HarperCollins*Publishers*,
77–85 Fulham Palace Road,
Hammersmith, London W6 8JB

A Paperback Original 1996
1 3 5 7 9 8 6 4 2

A catalogue record for this book
is available from the British Library

ISBN 0 00 638703 9

Set in Linotron Times by
Rowland Phototypesetting Limited,
Bury St Edmunds, Suffolk

Printed in Great Britain by
Caledonian International Book Manufacturer, Glasgow

CONTENTS

INTRODUCTION

When you save money, you usually pay tax on the interest or profits. That means you're paying tax twice – once when you earn the money, and once when you save it. Most of us meekly accept the right of the powers that be to extract this money from our building society accounts and other savings. It's only when you stop to think about it that you realize that it is both arbitrary and illogical for the government – any government – to do this to us.

Taxing our savings makes us more inclined to spend than save. Now if most of us were instinctive hoarders and misers, this might make sense. But the reality is that we are not, and that our economy – like most developed economies – is short of investment and therefore short of savings, because finance for investments like factories and new shops can only come from savings. So, logically, any government should want to encourage us all to save in order to promote investment and achieve greater economic growth.

The facts are otherwise. Ever since the end of the war in 1945 (during wars, savings are always encouraged, as long as you lend your money to the Government) successive governments have taxed savings. Today's tax rates, it is true, are lower than the colossal levels reached under the Labour administration in the 1970s, when the income tax rate on savings reached 98%, but they are still a deterrent to savings.

This seems all the more foolish when you consider how the safety net provisions of what used to be the Welfare State have been reduced in recent years. The State Old Age Pension now represents under a fifth of national average earnings and does not even pretend to provide a subsistence income. Most pensioners without other sources of income have to claim means-tested benefits, which have to be paid for by our taxes; but there'd be less need for them if people were encouraged to save more for their old age. Recent reductions in the automatic State protection of income when you are unemployed or sick also mean that you need a larger lump of savings to fall back on.

So there are excellent reasons why any British government should encourage savings, yet any such encouragement has been fragmented and often contradictory. Tax relief on the premiums paid towards life assurance policies – a major incentive to save and to provide protection for your family – was abolished in the 1980s. And despite a lot of rhetoric from the Conservative Government about 'level playing fields' (theoretically, equal tax treatment for all forms of saving), the simple and obvious answer – to exempt all savings from tax – has been rejected on the grounds that the Treasury would 'lose' too much tax revenue.

Instead, we have had a succession of new schemes giving tax incentives or exemptions to various forms of savings, so at least everyone has some opportunity to avoid tax. But, as independent research has shown, almost all these schemes are more widely and better used by the rich than by the poor: those who are worst off and have most to gain from a simple tax exemption on all savings are those who lose most from the current system.

This array of schemes has been set up by successive governments – or even successive ministers in the same government – to win political credit for supporting this or that cause. A politician may decide to encourage investment in small, brand-new companies, but it is not necessarily a good investment for you.

Overall, though, politicians have realized that we need to encourage savings: as the Treasury continues to oppose a simple, wide-ranging tax exemption, their answer has been the creation of a large number of schemes offering some sort of tax incentive or concession. The tax legislation covering all the schemes outlined in this book runs to thousands of pages, not to mention the jungle of schedules, qualifying rules, restrictions, terms and conditions that keeps armies of accountants and Inland Revenue administrators busy.

This mass of rules and regulations is of little interest to most people. The aim of this book is to help you to save and invest your money without paying tax twice – and without taking on too much risk or too many small print restrictions. In most of the areas covered, you should end up knowing whether a particular type of savings scheme is of interest to you, how it works and where you can get detailed information. If a married couple took advantage of the tax-exempt savings opportunities in just two of the available schemes, Personal Equity Plans and Tax Exempt Special Savings Accounts, then over a five-year period they could salt away £78,000 under the current rules, which with reasonable investment growth could be worth over £120,000. You don't need to emigrate to find tax havens – UK legislation has created several right here offering excellent opportunities whether you are looking for capital growth or income, low-risk or higher-risk, high-return investment.

In the interests of clarity, I have avoided as much jargon as possible. I have also drastically simplified the treatment of several highly technical and obscure areas of taxation like trusts in order to give an outline of what is possible. If you are interested in these more tricky areas you should certainly obtain guidance from a specialist before leaping into the fray.

1 || *Why Not Paying Tax on Your Savings Can Make You a Fortune*

Tax and Savings

Paying tax on your savings may not seem a big deal. Suppose you get, say, 4.8% net of tax instead of 6% tax-free. What's a mere 1.2%? Why worry about it? The Chancellor of the Exchequer would approve of such thinking – it enables him to collect billions of pounds from taxable accounts of all kinds without any irritating and noisy complaints from savers.

But look at it another way. Would you pay £12,000 for a car with no significant differences from another which cost only £10,000? When you are buying household goods, will you buy Product A for 20% more than nearly identical Product B? No and no. So why place your money in schemes where they pay tax when there are non-taxable schemes available?

But the situation isn't quite like that, because even though we've used the correct personal income tax rate to represent the difference in cost, the second example implies that the difference between the gross (before tax) and net (after tax) figures is 20%. Though this may be true as far as the Chancellor is concerned – at the lower tax rate applied to savings, he is collecting 20% of your income – from your point of view the figures are rather different: if you normally get 4.8%, but find a way of getting 6%, you increase your return not by a fifth but by a full 25%. So winning exemption from income tax on your savings actually boosts your return by a quarter.

Even so, whether the benefit you gain is 20% or 25%, you may think that the actual figure in this example – 1.2% – is too small to worry about. In fact, apparently small differences between the net, after-tax rate and the tax-free rate can make you a fortune over a period of years. This is due to the power of compound interest, a little-understood phenomenon which Albert Einstein once nominated as the most astounding feature of the world after relativity.

The effects of compound interest

'Simple interest' means the interest remains constant. Simple interest paid annually at 4.8% would mean interest of £48 on £1,000 year after year. Compound interest accumulates. At the end of the first year, the interest on £1,000 at 4.8% would be £48. But in the second year the interest would be earned on £1,048, so it would be £50.30. In the third year the interest earned on £1,098.30 would be £52.72. And so on.

Now think about the effect of compounding at 6% instead of 4.8% – and look at the way the figures in Table 1 diverge over time. After five years the difference between earning 4.8% and 6% on that initial £1,000 has reached £74, over 7% of the initial stake. After 10 years the difference is nearly £200. And it keeps on growing. Over time, not paying tax clearly does make a significant difference. Table 1 lists the figures for several different gross and net rates, all using the standard savings income tax rate of 20% as the difference. The higher the rate of return you earn on your money, the bigger the advantage you secure by not paying tax.

Table 1: How £1,000 grows tax-paid and tax-free

	Period in years			
	5	10	15	20
4.8% tax-paid	£1,264	£1,598	£2,020	£2,554
= 6% tax-free	£1,338	£1,791	£2,397	£3,207
8% tax-paid	£1,469	£2,159	£3,172	£4,661
= 10% tax-free	£1,610	£2,594	£4,177	£6,728
9.6% tax-paid	£1,581	£2,501	£3,955	£6,255
= 12% tax-free	£1,762	£3,106	£5,474	£9,646

The same effect on regular savings of a fixed monthly amount is shown in Table 2. This compares a fixed £100 per month saving in a net, taxable scheme with the same investment in a gross, tax-exempt scheme, at compound rates. The tax-exempt scheme pulls ahead over the years in a remarkable way.

Table 2: How £100 per month accumulates tax-paid and tax-free

	Period in years			
	5	10	15	20
8% tax-paid	£7,341	£18,128	£33,978	£57,266
= 10% tax-free	£7,717	£20,146	£40,162	£72,398
9.6% tax-paid	£7,641	£19,725	£38,839	£69,124
= 12% tax-free	£8,110	£22,404	£47,593	£91,985

Most of us have at least the occasional daydream along the lines of 'If I had £100,000 . . .' Table 3 tells you how long it would take you to accumulate that £100,000 from a regular monthly saving, again comparing taxable and tax-exempt schemes at different rates of interest. Taking a £200 per month saving at a 10% gross rate, the tax-exempt scheme wins the race by two and a half years. At 10%, your £200 per month reaches £100,000 in the 17th year, while at 8% the target is reached in the 20th year.

Table 3: How long it takes to accumulate £100,000 tax-paid and tax-free

Amount saved	Tax-paid interest rate	Number of years	Tax-free interest rate	Number of years
£100 per month	8%	26	10%	23
	9.6%	24	12%	21
£200 per month	8%	19	10%	16.7
	9.6%	17	12%	15.5
£500 per month	8%	11	10%	10
	9.6%	10.1	12%	9.4

As these examples and tables show, there are real benefits of escaping tax on your savings. Over just a year or two they may not seem substantial, but over a period of years they mount up and would make a big difference to your personal wealth and your freedom to pursue your goals in life. And, thanks to the varying enthusiasms of successive chancellors of the exchequer, there is now a large and potentially bewildering array of schemes with a variety of tax concessions, so you can use several of these schemes simultaneously – and there will often be good arguments for doing just this.

Diversification

Some types of saving will be more attractive than others, depending on your circumstances, but the principle of diversification also provides grounds for using different schemes. 'Diversification' is nowadays based on intensive mathematical investigations of the relationships between different markets and types of investment, but essentially it comes down to the old idea of not putting all your eggs in one basket. The experts now claim that if you invest in several different types of assets, you can increase the overall return you get on the money without an equivalent increase in risk. On the contrary, such extra returns can, they claim, often be earned without taking on any extra risk at all; in some situations you can even reduce the overall risk you run by adding a risky type of investment to your existing ones.

So don't confine yourself to one or other of the more obviously favourable types such as the popular Tax Exempt Special Savings Accounts (TESSAs) or personal pension plans. Casting your net wider can help you to shelter more of your money from the taxman and to create a better balanced set of investments for you.

Tax-free and tax-exempt

Most jargon terms will be explained as they arise, but there's one set that you'll need to be familiar with straight away: you might think that 'tax-free' and 'tax-exempt' mean exactly the same, but you could be wrong. And promoters of savings schemes always like to put the best gloss on their wares. 'Tax-exempt' means completely free of UK tax. You do not need to enter the purchase or sale of tax-exempt investments in your tax return; nor do you need to declare any income you draw from them. They are, effectively, outside the tax net completely – at least as far as the UK is concerned. Within the European Union, too, savings that are specifically exempted from tax in one country will normally be treated as tax-exempt in other countries, though anyone moving from one tax jurisdiction to another will need to check this.

'Tax-free' means that you pay no tax, but this may be for one of three reasons: the status of the investment itself, your own circumstances, or a combination of the two. For example, if you are a non-taxpayer – that is, your total income is less than the personal tax allowance you are entitled to – then the interest you get from a deposit account may be tax-free. But if your income were to exceed the relevant threshold, the interest would be taxable. So 'tax-free' may be a conditional description, whereas 'tax-exempt' is absolute and applies regardless of your personal circumstances.

'Tax paid' means that what you receive has had tax deducted from it. The return will usually be quoted 'net' or 'net of income tax'.

Tax-efficiency

Financial planners often use the term 'tax-efficient'. This is a relative term that takes your own circumstances into account. Any type of saving will be tax-efficient if it results in you paying less tax than you would otherwise have done. For tax planners – specialists who advise on how to reduce your tax bills – tax-efficiency can become a holy grail, to be pursued at all costs, but most financial planners try to see it in context. The restrictions imposed on tax-efficient deals may mean that you no longer have the flexibility or freedom you need with your cash. Nor should tax-efficiency alone justify the choice of investments: first decide on the type of investment you want, and *then* consider the most tax-efficient way of obtaining it.

The Changing Face of Saving

Savings versus investment

Back in the late nineteenth century, when the life assurance companies, friendly societies and building societies invented savings for the working classes, only the very rich had capital. So investment of capital, and savings of a penny a week in assurance policies (mainly to ensure that you had a decent burial) were completely separate.

This class-based distinction between savings and investments persisted right through until after 1945. The wealthier among the middle classes, with their growing affluence, participated in the stock market frenzy of 1927–9. Investment trusts had been invented in the 1860s to enable people with capital of some thousands of pounds (perhaps £100,000 today) to spread the risk of investing in the 'junk bonds' issued by risky and default-prone South American railroads and governments. When unit trusts were developed in the early 1930s those with modest sums (the equivalent of £5,000 or so today) were able to invest in shares – though this was still regarded as a very risky enterprise: most of the life assurance companies still held the bulk of their investments in gilt-edged securities.

Between 1900 and 1960 the world of savings was dominated by the life assurance companies and the building societies. The life assurance companies offered to the working class the penny-a-week or shilling-a-week burial policies through their 'industrial branch'. Through their 'ordinary branch' they offered with-profits policies, with a much higher investment content, to the middle classes. Payments – knowns as premiums – for industrial branch policies were collected door-to-door in cash on a weekly basis, while holders of ordinary branch policies paid through their bank accounts.

The ordinary branch with-profits policies offered by life assurers turned out to be very good investments from 1945 onwards, and the middle classes took to them with enthusiasm: these policies were regarded – in the era before occupational pension schemes – as the best possible way of accumulating a lump sum for retirement.

Even after 1945 the class distinction between savings and investment remained strong. The working classes took out industrial branch policies and made passbook savings with building societies. The middle classes took out ordinary branch policies and started to dabble in the stock market through unit trusts. Both the building societies and the life assurers formed cosy, oligopolistic cliques in which competition was minimal. The Welfare State provided cradle-to-grave support and, with one major exception – tax relief on premiums for life assurance policies – government support for savings was negligible. This tax relief was justified on the grounds that families benefiting from payouts from life assurance policies would not be a burden on the State. (This tax relief was withdrawn in 1982 but, given changing fashions in tax incentives, will probably be reintroduced before long.)

The process of change in the financial sector began in the 1960s with a wave of mergers between building societies, resulting in the dominance of the industry by the largest ten societies. Likewise the 'big four' clearing banks dominated the banking sector. The building societies remained firmly wedded to mortgage finance and, being restricted by legislation, failed to develop other forms of savings products for their customers.

Independent unit trust companies were launched in droves in the buoyant stock market conditions of the late 1960s and early 1970s. The 'small investor' could now get a share of the stock market action with a modest £250, and the newspapers were full of advertisements for these new and exciting investments – until the stock market crash of 1974.

Property

But throughout the 1960s, 1970s and most of the 1980s the middle classes were obsessed with one form of investment to the exclusion of all others: property. Residential property prices rose at a higher rate than retail prices, and property ownership was seen as the best defence against the erratic but mostly high inflation rates of this period. All you had to do was borrow money to buy the biggest house you could afford, move to a bigger house with a larger mortgage after a few years, and continue the process, and you would end up with a sizeable capital sum. This party came to an end with a drop of between 20% and 30% in property prices in the southern half of Britain between 1989 and 1994, and the hangover continues today: at the end of 1995 nearly a million homeowners were still caught in the 'negative equity trap'. The property boom also produced a boom in mortgage finance and contributed to a huge increase in the size of the building societies.

The end of the British love affair with property has important implications for savings. If you devote less of your monthly income to supporting a large mortgage, you have more to spend or save: and if you are given enough incentive to do so, you will save more. Financial assets such as shares now appear more attractive than property as a means to preserve capital against inflation and increase it.

Recent developments

Following the decline of mortgage finance and the deregulation of the financial services industry, competition between different types of financial concern started to increase in the late 1980s. The banks were offering investments in the form of unit trusts, and then went on to set up their own life assurance companies. The building societies won legislative freedoms to operate their own insurance companies and also started to offer a wider range of savings and investment products. The life assurers have been slow to respond to a changing environment: the life assurance industry remains fragmented and inefficient compared with banking or building societies. Even in 1995 some life assurers were still attempting to justify the maintenance of a separate industrial branch operation with costs accounting for as much as half of all the premiums collected – a certain recipe for poor value for money for their policyholders. But some life assurers have merged with banks, others with building societies, and further sweeping changes and rationalization through mergers and takeovers is likely in this sector.

The two most notable recent developments have been the erosion of the distinction between savings and investment and the increase in competition. Today many financial products double as savings and investment plans: you can invest lump sums or regular monthly amounts – the choice is yours. Such flexibility is certainly an advantage in the uncertain economic conditions of the 1990s. And with redundancy payments, lump sum pension fund payouts at retirement, maturity values of regular savings policies and inheritance all providing more people with capital sums, the range of plans and products available has increased substantially. Though competition is welcome, it does mean that you are faced with a greater choice than ever. To take only two examples, there are now over 700 different Personal Equity Plans and over 2,000 unit trusts available in the UK.

Until 1995 choosing between different savings and investment products was a nightmare. Providers of financial products were not required to provide simple comprehensible information on the costs built into the various products, so it was almost impossible to identify value for money. Thanks to new regulations that came into force in 1995, all providers of saving or investment products must give comparable data on their costs and charges, so that you can now directly compare one with another and see which represents best value for money. This is a major revolution in the financial services industry and is likely to sharpen the forces of competition still further as consumers learn to discriminate in favour of better-value products. This topic is covered in Chapter 10 (see page 132).

Here it is just worth noting that some of the 'mass market' savings and investment products being promoted to the public now offer better value for money than many financial services aimed at the very wealthy. So, as the end of the twentieth century approaches, financial services are at last starting to obey the normal laws of volume and price that apply to other consumer products: those that are produced and sold in the largest numbers offer the best value for money. You may find it surprising that market forces are only now starting to operate in this area, but savers and investors in the UK are better off, in terms of the variety of products, competition and information than those in the more heavily regulated and oligopolistic markets of some other European countries.

Your Returns from Saving and Investing

When you save or invest money you expect to get an immediate income or a future gain or both. Your income will come from interest or dividends, which you may either spend or put back into the plan (reinvest). Since one plan may produce interest only while another produces only capital gains and a third produces a mixture of these, how do you compare one with another?

Total return and reinvestment of income

The concept of total return is essential in comparing investments. Total return adds together the interest and any gains you get and expresses them as an annualized percentage of your initial capital or your monthly saving. If you invest £1,000, get 5% interest at the end of the year and also get a capital gain of 5% at the end of the year, then the total return is 10%. But suppose you reinvest the interest over a period of five years: what will the total return be then? In practice this will depend on the rate of interest you earn on the interest that you reinvest. Over a year or two, whether you get 3% or 8% on this reinvested interest will make little difference to the final sum you end up with, but over a period of 25 years the difference will be significant. Unless otherwise stated, it is always assumed that the rate of interest you get on reinvested interest will be the same as the original interest rate. So in the above example it would be assumed that interest would be earned on reinvested interest at a rate of 5%. This also applies to the rate of capital growth on any income or capital reinvested.

It is essential to do the sums in this way in order to compare the returns from one form of investment with those from another, but you should recognize that this picture does not necessarily correspond to reality, especially if you are making a lump sum investment in a fixed interest investment and reinvesting the interest. The actual rate earned on the reinvested interest will vary in line with interest rates at the time the reinvestments are made, and this could be a higher or lower rate than the original interest rate.

Reinvestment of income has been shown in the past to be an extremely important constituent of the high returns from stock market investment. And there is a big difference between reinvesting share dividends gross, without any tax paid, and investing them net of income tax – a difference that becomes very large indeed after a period of 25 years.

Charges

The other point to remember is that, as Tables 1 and 2 (see pages 6 and 7) show, a small difference in the rate of return over a long period can make a very large difference to the amount your plan is worth. Savings and investment plans offered by all types of financial institutions levy charges which directly reduce the return you get. A small saving in annual charges can therefore be worth a large extra sum of capital at the end of 15 or 20 years. For example, suppose you are trying to choose between two savings plans linked to shares. You are planning to save £100 per month over 15 years. Over this term we will assume that the annual return generated by the investments is 10%. One of the plans levies an annual charge of 1% while the other charges 1.5%. The payout from the first plan will be £36,930; the second plan with the higher charge pays only £35,520. In practice, the difference in charges is often much greater than this, so selecting good-value plans with lower charges can help you to improve the returns you get on your money.

A few long-established collective investment schemes levy

annual charges of under 0.5%; there are others which charge as much as 2.5% a year. In recent years managers have used a variety of excuses, such as an increase in regulatory costs, to steadily increase the annual charge levied on newly launched collective investment and savings schemes of every kind. Only very recently have there at last been welcome signs of competition leading to lower charges.

Despite managers' claims to expertise in investing your money, there is very little evidence that investment managers can add value to your investments at a rate of even 1% a year (i.e. by being directly responsible for your money earning an extra 1% a year on top of the norm for the relevant type of investment). Independent surveys of collective funds like unit trusts and pension funds have shown that while many management companies may achieve this every so often, over time no manager consistently does it year after year. Except in the unlikely event of your finding a manager with an exceptional record of consistent past results, or offering a scheme with particular and exclusive advantages, you should therefore be very wary of paying high annual charges.

As a result of new regulations on disclosure of charges, every savings and investment plan manager is obliged to provide you with an illustration showing the effect of charges on the amount accumulated in the plan. These are extremely useful documents that provide real comparative data on charges. Whatever plans you are considering, you should always look carefully at these figures and compare them to several other plans of the same type.

When comparing banks and building society accounts, the most useful comparative measure is the Compound Annual Rate or CAR. This takes into account the frequency of interest payments. For example, consider an account paying a gross interest rate of 8%. Table 4 shows the CAR if interest is paid once, twice, four times or twelve times during the year. The more often interest is paid or credited to the account, the more opportunity there is to earn interest on interest. If you compare accounts only on the basis of nominal interest rates, without taking into account frequency of interest payments, you could end up making the wrong choice. Bank and building society accounts normally quote the CAR and this is the best measure to use.

Table 4: The effects of compounding interest

Nominal interest rate: 8%	
Frequency of interest payments	*Compound annual rate (CAR)*
Yearly	8%
Six-monthly	8.16%
Three-monthly	8.24%
Monthly	8.30%

Whenever annual returns are referred to in this book, they are calculated on the same basis as the CAR: they are compound rates that allow for earning additional returns on both income and gains that are reinvested or held within the plan. Annual return is the term used in this book, but you may come across two other terms that have the same meaning: compound growth rate and internal rate of return.

2 ‖ *Know Your Enemy*

Before setting out to liberate your savings from the taxman, it is important to have a clear idea of the tax laws and how they affect the interest, dividends and profits you receive from your savings. You will then know what evasive action is necessary. For example, most people don't need to take specific steps to avoid capital gains tax, because few of us make full use of our annual gains exemption.

Income Tax

Income tax, though, is a different matter: most of us are liable to income tax on interest and dividends, and the tax is actually deducted at source before we even get our income. Essentially, all income from investments and savings is taxable unless it is specifically exempted by legislation, as in the case of many of the tax-favoured investments discussed later in the book (see pages 67–116).

Following tax changes in the 1993 and 1995 Budgets, there is now a difference between the rates of income tax you pay on your earnings on the one hand and on your savings and investments on the other. For earnings or pension income, tax is levied at 24% or 40%, while for income from savings and investments it is levied at 20% or 40%.

So long as your taxable income, including all income from savings and investments, is less than £25,500 (the level above which tax is payable at 40%), then all your investment income will bear tax at 20%. If your taxable income is over £25,500, then you will pay tax at 40% on the amount of your investment income that is above the £25,500 threshold.

In some cases, you may receive interest or dividends where tax at 20% has already been deducted from the income. In other cases you may receive income from which no tax has been deducted. In both cases the rule for working out how much tax you should pay is the same: you add the gross investment income to your earned or pension income. If this results in taxable income below £25,500, then if tax was deducted at source from your interest or dividends, you have no more to pay. If no tax was deducted at source, the law requires you to declare the income and pay 20% tax on it.

Bank and building society accounts
The biggest source of interest is bank and building society accounts: income tax at 20% will be deducted from all the interest paid unless you sign a declaration that you are a non-taxpayer, in which case you may receive your interest without deduction of tax. Children, for example, are almost always non-taxpayers and are entitled to receive interest gross (without tax deduction), though a parent must sign the declaration on their behalf.

For taxpayers, the tax is deducted from each interest payment from UK bank and building society accounts. The rules require you to include the gross amount of interest you have received during the tax year (6 April to 5 April) in your income when working out your tax liability. This may seem pointless, considering that you have already paid the tax, but the Inland Revenue wants to see if you are due to pay any more tax on top of what you have already paid. This will apply if the gross interest you receive, added to your other income, means that your total taxable income exceeds the threshold at which the higher rate of tax (40%) becomes payable (see Table 5, page 21). In this case you will be required to pay additional tax of 20% of the gross interest in excess of the threshold, because you will be liable to 40% tax but will only have paid 20%.

When doing your sums to work out your own estimated income and tax figures, always remember to 'gross up' any net payments of interest. If you know that you have received, say, £80 in net interest during the tax year, the grossed up amount, which is the figure the Inland Revenue will use to determine your taxable income, is £100.

UK Banks and building societies are not allowed to pay gross interest to UK taxpayers, but one major institution may do so: National Savings. Its Income Bond and Investment Account both pay interest without deduction of tax, which is handy for non-taxpayers. Those who pay tax must do so after declaring the income in their tax returns.

Fixed interest investments

The next major category of income from savings is interest from fixed interest investments such as the gilt-edged securities issued by the Government. Fixed interest securities issued by companies and municipalities (sometimes referred to as 'town hall bonds') come into the same category. Here, the normal procedure is for interest to be paid net of tax at 20%; non-taxpayers can reclaim the tax paid. In the case of gilts, if you buy them via the National Savings Stock Register (through post offices), then interest is paid without tax being deducted, though the interest must be included in your gross income and tax will be paid in due course.

Shares, unit and investment trusts

The tax treatment for all UK shares, unit and investment trusts is similar. Tax is again deducted at source from all dividend payments at 20%. The 'tax credit' on dividends – the amount companies are entitled to deduct in tax – is 20%, and provided your taxable income is below £25,500 (the higher rate threshold) you will have no further tax liability. However, if you pay tax at 40%, the Inland Revenue will demand a full extra 20% tax. And if you are a non-taxpayer, they will hand you back 20% if you put in a tax reclaim. To decide whether you are liable to 40% tax on dividends, the Inland Revenue regards any dividends you receive as the 'top slice' of your income.

Property

The tax treatment of the types of income mentioned above is relatively straightforward. Income from property is rather more complex, because – assuming you own property which is rented for profit – it is treated as business income. Various deductions may be made from the total income to arrive at the taxable income. These include interest on any loans you have taken out to acquire the property, maintenance and insurance costs and agents' fees. The rate of tax will be your normal income tax rate – 24% or 40%.

To sum up the income tax position: with most UK investments, a taxpayer has rate income tax at 20% deducted at source from the income. In most cases (except for assurance funds), a non-taxpayer may reclaim the tax that has been deducted, while those whose taxable income exceeds the higher rate income tax threshold will be liable to pay additional tax representing the difference between the tax deducted at 20% and their own personal liability at 40% – i.e. an extra 20%.

Table 5: Income tax allowances, rates and bands for 1995–96 and 1996–97

	1995–96	1996–97
Personal allowance	£3,525	£3,765
Married couples allowance*	£1,720	£1,790
20% tax rate: on income up to	£3,200	£3,900
24% tax rate: on income	£3,201–£24,300	£3,901–£25,500
40% tax rate: on income over	£24,300	£25,500
Annual exemption from capital gains tax	£6,000	£6,300
'Nil rate band' for inheritance tax	£154,000	£200,000

*This is no longer a genuine tax allowance. Only 15% of £1,790 may be offset against tax liability, regardless of your personal tax rate. The allowance is therefore worth a tax reduction of £268.50 to all taxpayers in 1996–97. Details of the age allowances will be found in Chapter 9 (see page 127).

The personal income tax allowances, the income tax rates and the bands of income to which they apply for the 1995–96 and 1996–97 tax years are shown in Table 5.

Since interest or dividends form the major part of the return from many forms of savings, it is clearly to your advantage to save or invest in ways that avoid tax on this income.

Capital Gains Tax

The second tax that affects your savings is capital gains tax. Because each taxpayer has an annual exemption of the first £6,300 of gains, relatively few people pay capital gains tax in any one year. Also, to avoid taxation of the 'paper profits' generated by inflation, the cost of investments is indexed: the actual price you paid is increased by the same percentage as the increase in the Retail Prices Index over the period for which you owned the asset, and only the profit *above* the resultant higher cost figure is potentially subject to tax – potentially, because it may still fall within your annual exemption.

Business assets benefit from many reliefs and exemptions from capital gains tax, so business owners can often find ways of escaping this tax, or at the very least deferring its payment. However, if you salt away a few thousand pounds year after year in investments and their value grows, and you then sell the assets all at once, you may find yourself with a capital gains tax bill. You may regularly acquire shares in the company you work for over a period of years: if the company does well and its shares rise in value, you may end up with a potential capital gains tax bill on just this one investment. Another category that can generate capital gains tax liabilities is the sale of second homes or investment properties after several years' ownership.

So while capital gains tax is not an everyday tax like income tax, it can nevertheless take a bite out of your savings, and the bite will be deep. This is because capital gains are taxed as if they were extra income. The gain, after allowing for indexation and deducting the annual exemption, is added to your income in the year of the sale. The tax you pay is the rate of income tax that would apply to this extra amount of income. So, to take an extreme case, if you made a gain after indexation of £1m then most of the gain would be taxed at 40% and the tax bill would be close to £400,000. Only if the gain is small enough so that your taxable income *plus* the gain is below the higher rate income tax threshold will the rate of tax on the gain be held to 24%.

Most of the assets you are likely to acquire through saving or investing are potentially subject to capital gains tax. It applies to all UK shares, investment trusts and unit trusts, offshore funds, and property (other than your own home). Unit and investment trusts pay no capital gains tax on the gains they make when the managers switch from one share to another, but when you sell your units or shares, any gain you make is potentially subject to tax.

Though capital gains tax is unlikely to be an immediate problem for most people, it is clearly worth thinking about how to prevent it becoming a problem in the future as it could take a large bite out of your profits.

Life Assurance Policies

The tax position for life assurance policies is different. The payouts from 'qualifying policies' – most policies for which regular premiums are paid for ten years or more, and all policies which provide only a pure life assurance benefit (such as term assurance) – are free of income tax and capital gains tax. But life assurance funds are themselves taxable. They pay tax at 20% on their income and at 24% on their capital gains.

The 'income' that you may draw from lump-sum life assurance policies has its own special tax regime. The term 'income' is used because, in their 'investment bonds', the life assurance companies do not normally distinguish between capital and income. You can make withdrawals from the policy, but while you may regard these withdrawals as income, they may in fact represent partial encashments of your capital.

But if we look at the operation of the life assurance funds, we find that UK life assurance companies pay tax at 20% on their income and at 24% on their capital gains. The tax is paid within the life assurance funds and cannot be reclaimed by an individual policyholder, even by a non-taxpayer. As regards income, then, life assurance funds are in no way a tax shelter for non-taxpayers or for standard-rate taxpayers; as far as capital gains tax is concerned, the position is worse, because each individual can make tax-free gains within his or her £6,300 annual gains exemption but all gains within life funds are taxable.

Higher-rate taxpayers investing in a life assurance fund incur the internal income tax rate of 20% in the life assurance fund, which is lower than the rate they would have borne if they owned the same investments personally. In effect they reduce their tax rate by 20%. But the reduction is temporary, because when a policy is encashed, the entire gain becomes potentially subject to higher rate tax. The gain over the period from the policy's inception is divided by the number of years the bond has been held, and the resultant sum is added to the investor's income in the year of encashment. The average rate of tax on this extra slice of income, less the standard rate of tax, is then applied to the whole gain. The deferment of the extra 20% tax may be worthwhile, though there are usually many other ways to achieve a similar deferment of both income tax and capital gains tax. But the tax situation of a higher rate taxpayer who makes a series of large withdrawals from a bond can be considerably more onerous than that just described.

UK life assurance policies, then, may offer 'tax-free payouts', and may also promote the fact that if you draw an income from the funds, you are not personally liable to tax. But since both income tax and capital gains tax are paid within life assurance funds, they cannot in any way be regarded as tax-free investments and they are not therefore covered in this book.

Inheritance Tax

The final tax you have to worry about is inheritance tax. Strictly speaking, it is your heirs who should do the worrying, since the tax is paid after death. But if you want to leave as much as possible of what you have built up to your chosen inheritors, you will probably need to give some thought to avoiding inheritance tax.

Inheritance tax is charged at a flat rate of 40% on all a person's taxable assets on death in excess of £200,000. There are many concessions and reliefs, but most of them apply to business assets. If your estate consists of a house, its contents and investments, then no reliefs will apply, so your inheritors will be faced with a tax demand for 40% of everything in excess of £200,000. Worse still, they will not be allowed to lay their hands on any of the cash, investments or property in your estate until they have paid this tax.

Fortunately there are ways in which you can avoid the tax partially or completely.

Some Obvious Loopholes in the Tax Net

The tax system is comprehensive, but there are loopholes in the tax net. This means there are legitimate ways of reducing the tax you pay on your savings even without making use of tax-favoured schemes. In this section we will look at three of them.

Taxation and married couples

In 1990 the basis of taxation of married couples – hitherto largely a joint one – was changed to the new independent arrangement. In almost all respects husband and wife are now taxed as individuals. This has important implications for savings and investments and can provide scope for useful tax savings.

Both husband and wife have their own personal allowance. The married couples allowance is no longer a real tax allowance but a tax credit offset against the husband's income tax liability. If the husband has no tax liability, it can be transferred to the wife and offset against her income tax liability.

The income from savings and investments owned by husband or wife individually is taxed as their personal income. With jointly owned assets the income is divided equally between them. It is possible to elect for the income from a jointly owned asset to be allocated in different proportions. For example, if a couple have a joint building society account, they may elect for 80% of the income to be treated as the wife's.

Capital gains tax applies on a similar basis. Gains accrue individually to personally owned assets, and are divided equally if they derive from jointly owned assets, though again an election may be made to change the proportions of ownership.

The tax-saving opportunities on savings and investments arise when husband and wife have different levels of earned or pension income – a common situation – and are therefore subject to different income tax rates. Wives often have several years without earned income when they are bringing up children, in which case they may have a personal tax allowance with no income to use it against.

Here are some examples of husband-and-wife situations where altering the ownership of savings and investments results in reducing the amount of income tax paid.

Example (1):
The non-earning wife

Julie has given up her job and has just had her first child. She intends to return to work in about three years after having a second child. She has no earned income. She and her husband Lionel have a joint building society account containing £10,000. The interest (paid net of tax) is divided equally for tax purposes. The husband has a separate building society account in his name containing £12,000, where the interest is also paid net.

If Lionel closes his building society account and a new one is opened in Julie's name, the interest will escape tax. Likewise, if they close the joint account and open a new one in Julie's name, this interest too will escape tax. Note that in this case, the couple could not usefully elect to have most of the interest from the joint account treated as hers. This is because with a joint account, interest cannot be paid without deduction of tax if one of the account holders is a taxpayer. Since Lionel is a taxpayer, interest from a joint account must be paid net. But as Julie is a non-taxpayer, she can sign the declaration on her own personal account and have her interest paid gross.

By doing this the couple will avoid 20% tax on their interest and so long as Julie's income remains within her personal allowance the interest will be tax-free.

Example (2):
The lower tax rate

Karen has restarted part-time work while the children are young. Her annual earnings amount to just over £5,000. Her husband Peter has a highly paid job and pays tax at 40% on £3,000 of his income. The couple have a joint building society account containing £14,000, with the interest divided equally between them. Peter has a separate building society account containing £8,000 and shares producing a gross annual income of £600. Because Karen's gross income is less than £7,665 she pays tax at 20%. If the couple close the building society accounts and open a new one in Karen's name, they will reduce the tax rate on the interest to 20%. Likewise, if Peter transfers the shares to Karen, the tax rate on the dividends will fall from 40% to 20%.

Example (3):
The windfall gain

Ken works for a company that went public 10 years ago, offering its shares on the stock market. He bought a large number of shares in the public offer on special terms, and since then has been buying shares through an employee share ownership scheme. The company has now accepted a takeover bid with the result that he will make a capital gain of £21,300 (after indexation) on his shares. Because he already pays tax at 40% on some of his income, the tax rate on the £15,000 taxable gain will also be 40%.

His wife Anne earns £12,000 a year and pays tax at 24%. If Ken transfers all the shares to Anne before the takeover goes through, then she will be regarded as having bought the shares for the same cost as Ken did, and will therefore make the £15,000 gain he would have done. But because Anne's taxable income will remain below the higher rate threshold, the tax rate on her gain will be 24% instead of 40%, saving £2,400 in tax.

Example (4):
Looking ahead to the family
Jean is in a well-paid job and pays tax at 40% on some of her income. She plans to stop work in about four years' time to have a family, and intends to be a full-time non-earning mother for at least two years. Her husband Luke is a standard-rate taxpayer. Between them they have £25,000 in building society accounts and she plans to save at least an extra £25,000 in the next four years, which she plans to draw on while she is not working.

Provided the couple do not want to spend the interest in the next four years, they can escape tax on it by placing money in Jean's name in a Channel Islands money fund. The fund is divided into shares and all the interest accumulates without any tax being deducted. When shares are sold, the accumulated interest becomes liable to UK tax. This means that Jean can encash the shares in the years when she has no other income, and thus avoid paying any tax at all on the interest.

As these examples show, independent taxation gives plenty of scope for reducing the tax you pay on your savings if you are alert to the opportunities. The special case of avoiding tax on savings for older people who may fall into the 'age allowance trap' is covered in Chapter 9 (see page 126).

Working abroad

A second major loophole in the tax net benefits those who work abroad. This only applies if you are working outside the UK full-time and you are abroad for more than a full tax year. In this case, you will only have to pay UK tax if you put your money into savings within the UK. So long as your normal place of residence is in the UK, which will be the case if you still own a home in the UK, you will be liable to tax on any UK income. But if you use savings schemes that are located in tax-free territories such as the Channel Islands, the Isle of Man or Luxembourg your income will not be subject to UK tax. Other countries' tax systems are different from ours, but in many cases, if you put savings into these tax-free zones, you will have no immediate tax liability in your country of temporary residence.

If you do take a job abroad, it is clearly worth moving your existing savings 'offshore' into tax-free territories. If either husband or wife has such a job while the partner stays in the UK, it can pay to transfer all the savings to the partner who is abroad so that they can be liberated from UK tax.

On returning to the UK, all the income and capital gains from your savings become taxable again, regardless of where the money is held. So it is as well to review the position before you return to see if you can avoid future UK tax through some specialized offshore investments. The range of offshore tax-free opportunities is discussed in Chapter 8 (see page 119).

Children

A third category of tax loophole concerns children. The current system gives each child his or her own personal income tax allowance, at the same level as for adults, from birth. Very few children under the age of 16 ever have more than a token amount of earned income, so most of this tax allowance – even allowing for the interest from the modest sums children may hold in bank or building society accounts – usually remains unused. Being non-taxpayers, children are entitled to receive interest without deduction of tax.

But the Inland Revenue thinks of everything. To prevent you using your children as a convenient 'tax shelter' and putting all your savings in their names so that the income escapes tax, it has a rule that if the investment income a child gets from money given by a parent exceeds £100 per year, then this income will be taxed as if it were the parent's. This does not prevent grandparents or other fond relatives from giving a child a handsome stack of savings which can remain tax-free. The rule only applies to parents.

Even this does not quite rule out the possibility of using a child as a tax shelter. You can make gifts to children of assets on which you have large accumulated gains and which qualify for 'holdover relief'. When you make a gift subject to holdover, any liability to tax is deferred until the asset is sold and is then payable by the donee, who takes over the asset at the same cost at which it was acquired by the donor. The relief is restricted to business assets but these include unquoted shares and shares listed on the Alternative Investment Market. If you do undertake sophisticated tax avoidance schemes of this type, the Inland Revenue will probably start to demand tax returns from the child and may question whether you had any right to get the money back from your young capitalist, so such activities need to be planned with great care.

On the whole it may be better simply to encourage children to save for themselves, even though few of them will appreciate their temporary freedom from the attentions of the Inland Revenue.

The fourth category of loophole – the one covered in the rest of this book – is saving and investment schemes that are tax-exempt or tax-free.

3 || *Setting the Right Aims for Your Savings*

There is no point in putting your money into tax-free savings if these produce a worse return than schemes where tax is paid. Nor should you accept the restrictions that often accompany tax-exempt schemes if these conflict with your likely future needs for cash.

These two points may seem obvious but each year they cause grief and financial loss to thousands of savers. Promoters of savings schemes are certainly partly to blame. They are rarely as open and honest about the restrictions or the early encashment penalties as they ought to be. Moreover, the advantages of tax-exemption are often given far more emphasis than promoters' charges that eat into the benefits of escaping the tax net, or the risks involved in some forms of tax-free saving. But savers too must bear some responsibility: many are too greedy or short-sighted and, most importantly, unrealistic in their objectives.

Savings and investments can build up capital for the future, but for many people – certainly those with family responsibilities – savings should take second place to protection. Saving £100 a month may make you rich in 20 years' time, but what would happen to your family if you were to drop dead tomorrow? Protection is a large subject in its own right, too large to cover here, but you should be confident you have dealt with this satisfactorily before you start thinking about saving or investing to build up capital for the future.

A good starting point when you come to plan your savings strategy is to ask yourself these questions about your savings:

- What is the money going to be used for in the future? How likely is it that you could use the cash for something else?
- When will you need to draw cash out?
- What are the chances of cash being needed earlier than this?
- Will you want to draw out a regular income, occasional lump sums or to cash the whole lot in?
- Are you going to take a low-risk, moderate-risk or high-risk approach? Or are you prepared for high risk on only some of your money? How much of it?
- Are you likely to be a taxpayer throughout the period up to your target date? Is your taxable income, and hence your tax rate, more likely to rise or fall?
- How much control do you want to have over your money? Do you want to handle most decisions yourself or are you prepared to entrust your cash to others to look after?
- Are your circumstances likely to change significantly in the next few years? If they did change, how many of the previous questions might you answer differently?

Serious consideration of the last question should make you wary of commitments to long-term, inflexible plans with large penalties for early encashment. Many more savers have lost money or obtained very poor returns from such plans than have profited substantially from them. The single most important factor in improving the return you get on your savings is to avoid early encashment of long-term contractual plans. The savings industry is moving away from long-term contractual commitments, but many plans of this type still exist. The longer the term of a contract, the more restrictive its terms, the higher its penalties if you quit early, and the more confident you need to be about your ability to stick with it right to the end. All this strongly suggests that you should never commit more than a small proportion of your savings to plans of this type.

Flexibility, then, is a great virtue in savings plans. It is a term that is routinely abused by savings promoters, who are quite capable of describing as flexible plans which have quite onerous contractual requirements. Flexibility is not a label – it is (or more often isn't) in the small print. Given your expected requirements for a regular income, irregular withdrawals – or possibly a combination of these – you need to read this small print to ensure you do have the flexibility that you want.

Setting Savings Aims

Many people save just because they feel it's a good idea to salt a bit of cash away. Many more, though, need an objective to motivate them to save money. 'More income in retirement' is probably the single most important objective set by savers in their 40s and 50s. Younger savers are more likely to see buying a house or providing for children – or their education – as their priorities. As for those over retirement age, their aim may be to leave a good inheritance for their children and grandchildren.

Once you start to think about it, you may realize that you have several different aims. Perhaps it's not just a question of 'more income in retirement': you may want a lump sum to make a special trip when you are 60, or to help your son or daughter when they get married.

If you have several different aims, you then have to prioritize them. Almost certainly you won't have enough money to meet all the aims you could set, so you will have to scale back your expectations or even drop one of your aims.

Aims and means

There are two ways of relating your aims to your means. The first is to say that you want to have a sum of, say, £50,000 in 15 years' time, and then work out – using the data in Table 6 (see page 35) – how much you need to save each month to get there. Or you can provisionally allocate a monthly sum to save and then work out (again from Table 6) how much it would grow in 15 years. The first method will probably produce a required monthly saving figure that is larger than you can afford; the second will probably produce a lump sum that is less than you want. So you will then need to adjust both figures and repeat the exercise, until you reach a savings figure you can afford that will produce a lump sum that you consider large enough.

For example, you might say you'd like to have £25,000 at the end of 10 years on the assumption that you use a moderate-risk scheme. Over 10 years, £100 a month in such a scheme produces £20,146, so it will take (25,000 ÷ 20,146 × 100 =) £124 per month to accumulate £25,000. You cannot really afford this, but you know you could afford £75 a month. In a moderate-risk scheme, £75 a month will produce (£20,146 × 75 ÷ 100 =) £15,111 at the end of 10 years. So you think again and decide you could afford to save £110 a month, which will accumulate (£20,146 × 110 ÷ 100 =) £22,160 over the same period.

As we saw earlier, an apparently small difference in the rate of return can make a big difference to the lump sum accumulated from the same regular saving over a period of years. Broadly, you would expect to earn a higher rate of return on the riskier types of investment and a lower rate on the less risky, and experience confirms this. Table 6 sets out what have historically been average rates of return from low-risk, moderate-risk and high-risk investments. The table shows the amounts you would accumulate from a given monthly saving at the middle rate for each of the three bands. This will enable you to calculate your savings needs.

The figures in Table 6 emphasize the compounding effects of accumulating at a higher rate of return. Over 25 years you could reasonably expect to receive almost four times as large a lump sum from a high-risk as from a low-risk scheme, so think hard about just how much risk you are prepared to take. Clearly, if you can take more risk, the extra return is well worth while.

Incidentally, though these figures may appear arbitrary – they are just compound interest figures, after all – there is plenty of evidence that savings schemes of the three types can and do deliver these returns. Some of this data is included in Chapter 10 (see page 136).

Table 6: Expected rates of return from low-risk, moderate-risk and high-risk savings

Risk type	Low	Moderate	High
Band of annual returns	5–8%	8–12%	12–18%
Central rate within band	6.5%	10%	15%
Sum accumulated from saving of £100 per month at central rate over			
3 years	£3,973	£4,184	£4,498
5 years	£7,071	£7,717	£8,734
7 years	£10,584	£11,992	£14,336
10 years	£16,758	£20,146	£26,302
13 years	£24,216	£30,998	£44,500
15 years	£30,031	£40,162	£61,635
17 years	£36,626	£51,251	£84,299
20 years	£48,215	£72,398	£132,707
25 years	£73,130	£124,316	£275,656

Deciding how much risk you can take with your savings requires an understanding of the basic nature of the investments your money will go into.

Investments and Risk

There are six distinct classes of investment, each with its own characteristics: deposits, fixed interest, indexed (or inflation-proof), equities, tangibles and derivatives. The most important features of each of these investments relate to credit risk, capital risk, income risk, and volatility.

Deposits

Deposits at a variable rate of interest are bank and building society accounts and some National Savings accounts. The capital is fixed and the interest varies in line with short-term interest rates generally. Since the capital is fixed, all the return comes in the form of interest. If you invest in National Savings, there is no credit risk: National Savings is a Government department and cannot go bankrupt. If you invest in the Onebranch Bank, there may well be a credit risk – small banks can and do go bust. The smaller and weaker the institution, the higher the rate of interest it will have to offer to attract savers to deposit money. All deposits have an element of capital risk, in that the capital is fixed and is eroded by inflation. The higher the rate of inflation, the greater the rate of capital erosion. The income risk in a deposit is that you do not know what rate of interest you will get in future. Short-term interest rates are one of the key economic levers that governments use in managing the economy. If there is a runaway boom (as at the end of the 1980s), then high rates of interest (as in the early 1990s) may be needed to bring it to a stop. If there is a deep recession (as in 1991–92), then very low interest rates may be needed to encourage consumers to borrow and spend. Because the capital is fixed, there is no volatility with deposits.

Given the strength of the lobbies in favour of low rates, no government ever wants short-term interest rates to be higher than is strictly necessary to prevent the economy misbehaving, so you would not normally expect to get a good return from deposits. But between 1990 and 1995 the real rate of short-term interest (the short-term rate minus the latest year-on-year rate of inflation) has been high, probably because of the prolonged aftermath of the huge credit binge of the late 1980s. You can work out the real net rate of interest from Figure 1 (see page 162); simply deduct the inflation rate from the buliding society interest rate on the same date. In any economy where inflation is low and everyone expects it to stay low, you would expect the short-term interest rate to be no more than 2% or so above the rate of inflation.

In the long run, the historical evidence is that deposits show a very poor rate of return as compared with fixed interest and equities. They are therefore suitable for short-term savings plans but are very rarely appropriate for savings terms of more than a few years.

Fixed interest investments

With fixed interest investments you get a fixed rate of income on your investment, usually for a fixed period of time. With some fixed interest investments you get your original capital back at the end of this agreed term. With others you may get a capital gain or loss if you hold your investment to maturity. Credit risk with fixed interest ranges from nil if you lend your money to the Government by investing in National Savings or buying gilt-edged securities, to high if you buy the fixed interest securities issued by a small company that is heading for the rocks. Like deposits, fixed interest investments have capital risk because they are vulnerable to inflation. In fact they are more vulnerable, because usually your money is committed for a period of years and if the rate of inflation rises sharply there is nothing you can do about it, whereas at least you can move your money out of a deposit. The income risk with fixed interest investments from reputable institutions is negligible. With fixed interest investments that are quoted on the stock market, like gilt-edged securities, there is volatility – prices vary from day to day depending on changes in the rate of inflation, movements in the exchange rate and other factors. The volatility is related to the remaining life of a fixed interest investment. If it is due to be redeemed within a year, then even a big change in the general level of interest rates will have little effect on its market price, but if the investment is not due to be redeemed for 10 years, then its price will move considerably more.

Most of the return from fixed interest investments comes in the form of interest. With stock market quoted investments there may also be capital gains if interest rates fall, though over a long period such gains are unlikely.

The period between 1945 and 1990 was generally a very bad one for fixed interest investment because of rising inflation (Figure 2, see page 163). Fixed interest as an investment does best when inflation is low and stable, and it is no coincidence that the Germans, who are used to low inflation, also invest far more in fixed interest than the British. Since 1990, though, gilt-edged and other fixed interest investments have produced much better returns, and if inflation stays low they may also prove a good investment in the future.

Indexed or inflation-proof investments

Indexed or inflation-proof investments are rare – there are only really two of them in the UK, both provided by the Government. This is logical since only the Government can control the rate of inflation. With the Government backing, there is no credit risk, nor is there any capital risk. There is income risk, since indexed investments pay a very low rate of interest above the rate of inflation. If the rate of inflation fell to zero, you would end up with a very low return, lower than you might obtain from other investments. With the indexed investments quoted on the stock market, there is also volatility. The price of these investments will tend to rise if investors anticipate a rise in the rate of inflation and fall if they expect a drop in inflation.

When inflation is low and relatively stable, indexed investments are not likely to perform well. But they are a 'hedge' against a sudden rise in the rate of inflation in the future.

Equities

'Equities' is the generic term for shares, and for other investments whose capital value and income can fall as well as rise. Shares involve credit risk, because companies can and do go bust. This very rarely happens to the largest 'blue chip' concerns, and is almost impossible with some categories of company such as utilities. So there is a range of credit risk between large, old-established, blue chips and small, newly formed companies where the risks of failure are greatest. Shares also involve capital risk though the evidence is that shares weather inflation better than other investments. There is income risk, because even if a company does not go bust it may cut its dividends. And shares are volatile, with prices moving sharply in response not just to news of profits and takeovers but to changes in interest rates and a host of other factors.

The returns from shares come partly in the form of dividends and partly in the form of capital gains. During the 1980s, of a total gross return from shares of 15% a year, roughly 5% came from dividends and the rest from capital gains.

Along with the higher risks from shares come higher returns. History shows that shares have handsomely outpaced deposits and fixed interest over the long term. The returns from deposits, fixed interest and equities are summarized in Table 7 and illustrated in Figure 3 (see page 164). The superior returns from shares explain why long-term investors, such as life assurance and pension funds, hold such a large percentage of their assets (over 75%) in shares.

Table 7: The long-term returns from deposits, fixed interest and equity investment

	Average annual returns from 1919–94	
	NOMINAL	REAL
Cash (Treasury bills)	5.4%	1.4%
Gilt-edged	5.7%	1.8%
Equity (shares)	11.9%	7.7%

The real return is the annual return in excess of the rate of inflation.

Source: BZW Equity-Gilt Study, 40th Edition

Property is a sub-category of equity investment, since both the capital value and the income can fall. With property there is rarely any credit risk in a developed economy like the UK, where disputes over the actual ownership of a property are fairly rare. But there is capital risk, which is increased by the costs of maintenance and repair – costs which may not be reflected either in an increase in market value or in the rental income it can generate. There is also income risk, aggravated by the fact that as an owner, you have to go on paying fire insurance premiums whether or not you have a rental income from a tenant. Both income risk and volatility are harder to assess for property than for shares since there is no central marketplace where prices are set.

From 1945 to 1988 residential property was an excellent investment, but since then it has fallen from favour in the wake of a major slump in prices. It is also an inflexible investment, difficult to sell, and the transaction costs of buying and selling are high compared with those of stock market investments.

Commercial property is a highly cyclical investment, with prices tending to peak when interest rates reach a low point and fall or slump as the new buildings financed with this cheap money become available for occupation.

Tangibles

Tangibles is the generic name for objects which may be regarded as investments. The common characteristic of things like stamp collections, coins, modern art, antiques, classic cars, gemstones, porcelain figurines, Japanese prints, gold bars, Russian lacquer miniatures, first editions of books and many, many more is that they produce no income. Indeed, if you insure them, tangibles make you pay to own them, whereas investments pay you to own them.

Tangibles are subject to a form of credit risk in that original items can be faked. There is an element of capital risk, though in the long run tangibles have shown themselves fairly inflation-proof. There is income risk in the form of the carrying cost of ownership represented by insurance and security. And changing fashions are responsible for a high degree of volatility in prices, not on a day-to-day basis but over a period of a few years.

The lack of reliable price data means it is hard to assess the performance of tangibles, but auction prices suggest that the best-quality items in many fields have performed well in financial terms over the long term, though not as well as shares.

Derivatives

Derivatives are financial instruments which give a return based on the performance of another type of assets (such as shares or property), an index (such as an index of share prices), or an interest rate or exchange rate. Most derivatives are short-term contracts traded on special exchanges. They are a highly unsuitable form of investment for your savings. However, they are increasingly used by professional investment managers either to reduce the risk involved in investing in shares, or to generate a higher income from a share portfolio, or to provide a guarantee that an investment in shares over a fixed period will not lose you money. And there is one category of derivatives – warrants to subscribe for shares – that do have a longer life, are available to individual savers, and can provide spectacular returns in exchange for equally spectacular risks.

You may choose to invest in residential property and tangibles off your own bat. Almost all the investments and savings offered by financial institutions are composed of deposits, fixed interest, equity or derivatives. Some are simple; others consist of a packaging of two or more of the three classes of investment.

Broadly speaking, deposits and some fixed interest investments are low-risk; some forms of fixed interest and many forms of equity investment involve moderate risk; and many more forms of equity investment involve high risk.

More Can Be Better

Each of the three main types of investment has its own characteristic risks and is therefore affected by particular events. Fixed interest is especially vulnerable to inflation and any rise in the inflation rate usually sends fixed interest investors running for cover. But shares normally take any change in inflation in their stride. A rise in short-term interest rates is good news for deposit-holders, who will get more interest – but it will normally be bad news for shares, since higher interest rates cut back economic growth, which could reduce profits and dividends. A fall in the rate of inflation is especially good news for fixed interest. A fall in the Sterling exchange rate is bad news for fixed interest but is often good for shares – because so many companies earn a large part of their profits overseas and those profits will translate into more pounds – and for indexed investments, because a drop in the exchange rate usually leads to a rise in the rate of inflation.

Given the unpredictability of future events, if you have some money in each of the three main types of investment, you will clearly damp down your overall level of risk – defined here as the tendency for the value of your savings to vary on a day-to-day basis. This is the basis of 'diversification', a grand name for the old and wise strategy of not putting all your eggs in one basket.

Your own future requirements for cash – the fact that you may need to draw some money from your savings in three years' time, some more in 10 years' time and yet more in 20 years' time – also means you need to consider different types of savings plan. Clearly it does not make good sense to start a high-risk savings plan if you need the cash in two years: the stock market may take a dive just when you need the cash. On the other hand, if you are pretty confident that you can commit part of your savings for 15 years, then the higher returns from equity-linked savings plans are likely to outweigh the extra risk. Even if the stock market does take a dive towards the end of the 15 years, the chances are that your plan will still end up ahead of other types of investment. Look at Table 6 (page 35) again – after 20 years you could see a 20% drop in the value of your equity plan and still be way ahead of the alternatives.

So your own future cash requirements and the logic of diversification both point to the merits of having savings plans with different levels of risk. All three of the major types of investment – and many combinations of them – are available in tax-free form. So you can choose from a wide menu while still ensuring that the taxman does not tuck into your meal.

For most people, saving for retirement is the single most important saving objective. So our survey of tax-free plans will start with pension plans, which benefit from the largest set of tax concessions.

4 ‖ Tax-efficient Savings for Your Retirement

The single biggest cause of financial anxiety is the question of income in retirement. Increasing job mobility, a shorter working life, erosion of State provision, increased expectations of retirement lifestyle and a longer average life expectancy have all contributed to the worry that we won't have enough in our old age.

How Big a Pension Do you Need?

Financial planners normally suggest that your retirement income should be two-thirds to three-quarters of your earned income in the years preceding retirement. This takes account of a reduction in some expenditures such as travel to work and purchase of clothes for work. If you no longer use your car to get to work every day your mileage will be reduced and you will not need to replace your car so often. On the other hand, when you retire you may well spend – or want to spend – more on your hobbies, interests and travel. One thing is certain: you will not find you have too much money if you have a retirement income of three-quarters of your pre-retirement earnings. But if you had to survive in retirement on a third of your former earned income, how would you cope?

The issue of retirement savings has been given more urgency by recent changes in the pattern of work and a reduction in the pension provided by the State. Fewer and fewer people are working from the ages of 16 to 65 – a common pattern not so long ago. Anyone coming on to the job market today is likely to be aged 21 or 22 after completing a college course. And even though officially pension age for men and women has been equalized at 65, fewer and fewer people retire at that age. Retirement at 60 is common in many large companies and 'early retirement' – which may be voluntary or forced – between the ages of 55 and 60 is taken by a significant minority of employees.

State pension provision

At the same time as people's working life has been shortening, the pension provided by the State has been shrinking. The flat-rate Old Age Pension now represents under 20% of national average earnings. Because earnings tend to rise at a faster rate than prices year after year, while the OAP is linked to the Retail Prices Index, it is certain that it will continue to shrink. By the year 2010 it could well be less than 10% of average earnings. You also need to have made National Insurance contributions for 90% of your working life to qualify for the full pension; otherwise you will get a reduced pension.

The contribution made by the State Earnings-Related Pension Scheme (SERPS) to today's workers' pensions is also uncertain, because the pension entitlements earned by anyone retiring after 1999 from SERPS have already been cut once by the Government. And projections of the costs of SERPS into the next century suggest they may have to be cut again to prevent a rising burden of taxes to pay for them.

In theory, if you retire after 2010, Serps should provide – on top of the flat-rate State pension – a retirement income of 20% of your average earnings from employment within the lower and upper National Insurance bands (for 1996–97: £3,172 and £23,660). Your earnings will be averaged over your entire working life, which obviously deflates the amount payable. (The original scheme based the pension on the average of your earnings over the highest-earning 10-year period during your working life, but the new formula is one of the changes designed to reduce the amounts paid out by the State.) Skipping some of the horrendous complexities of SERPS, the limitation of the maximum pension to 20% of the upper earnings on which National Insurance contributions are paid means that currently the maximum possible SERPS pension is about £100 per week, an amount which will probably rise roughly in line with average earnings over the years.

There are major question marks over SERPS, however. In 1988 the Government encouraged workers to 'contract out' of SERPS by offering to pay rebates of their National Insurance contributions into private pension plans taken out as SERPS substitutes. Not only did these rebates vastly exceed original estimates, thus negating the supposed cost advantage for the Government, but many of the private pension plans that were used solely as SERPS substitutes have such high charges that those who made the transfer could be worse off as a result. Since the transferees have the right to opt back into SERPS again, creating new future liabilities for the State, the whole issue remains a potential time bomb which is clearly going to require further remedial action from the Government. But you can be fairly sure that such action will not involve any improvement in the benefits provided by SERPS, and in any case self-employed people get no SERPS entitlement.

So to sum up the State's likely role in providing your retirement income, the flat-rate OAP might provide about 10% of national average earnings for anyone retiring after 2010, while if you contribute to SERPS, this might provide a further amount representing between 5% and 15% of national average earnings, taking account of the 'lifetime' averaging factor.

Because these figures all relate to national average earnings, they will represent a lower percentage of your earnings if you earn more than the national average.

Occupational pension schemes

In addition to the State pension schemes, most employees are also members of occupational pension schemes. There are two types: defined benefits (or final salary) and defined contributions (also known as money purchase). Most schemes are contributory:

members pay a small percentage of their earnings into the scheme, while employers pay in a larger sum.

In a defined benefit scheme, you accrue pension rights at a set rate each year, often on the basis of one 60th of your earnings per year. These pension rights are in relation to your final salary, so such schemes offer a good deal to those who remain with the same employer until retirement age. The deal is not so good for those who move jobs frequently since the pension rights are fixed in relation to your earnings when you leave the employment, and what these rights are worth at any time is based on a number of obscure factors. You have to choose between leaving the pension rights with the former employer, where they will escalate in line with prices, up to a maximum of 5% a year; transferring them into the new employer's scheme, where the rights may be worth less than they were in the original employer's scheme; or transferring them into an independent personal pension plan, where their growth rate up to retirement will depend on investment performance of the plan. If you retire earlier than the scheme's normal retirement age, your pension will be reduced.

In a defined contribution scheme, the employee's and employer's contributions go into a separate account for each individual. The contributions are invested and the accumulated capital sum is used to purchase pension income at retirement. When you change jobs, the current value of the account moves with you, either to your new employer's scheme or into a personal pension plan.

With both types of scheme, you may take part of the accumulated fund (the maximum is 1.5 times your final salary) as a tax-free lump sum at retirement together with a lower pension.

By now you will be starting to appreciate how difficult it is to come up with a simple formula telling you how much you need to save to achieve that three-quarters of pre-retirement earnings target. We are struggling towards a rough and ready formula, but first we need to cover a couple more factors.

Inflation

Over periods of 25 years compound interest rates of 12% or so create telephone-number payouts from even modest monthly savings, but what do these figures mean? What will the money buy in 25 years' time? It is difficult to say because we do not know what the rate of inflation will be. We need to take inflation out of the calculations so that you can relate what you may get from your savings to your income.

The relationship between the rate of return you get on your savings and the rate of inflation is not fixed, so we will have to make an assumption. The assumption, based on historical evidence, is that Equity investments over the long term will earn an average real rate of return (a rate of return on top of inflation) of 5% a year. (In fact, the long-term average is higher than this – 7.7% a year – so the assumption is conservative.) Using this assumption we can relate today's saving to today's salary. We can say that if you save £100 per month for 20 years you will end up with £40,750 and this amount is directly comparable, in spending power terms, with your current earnings.

Capital and income

But we also need to establish a relationship between the capital built up by savings and the income this capital will generate, since it is the income you are interested in.

There are two ways we could do this. We could ask what rate of income you could draw from a capital sum without eroding the capital value, so that your pension income represented just the income earned from the capital sum. Or we could ask how long you were going to live for and convert the capital sum, as well as the interest it earned, into a pension income. These two methods will produce very different answers.

Suppose you could get a 7% income without eating into your capital. Then to provide an income of £10,000 a year you would need a capital sum of £143,000. But for a man aged 60, conversion of the capital into income through the purchase of an annuity would provide an income of 12% guaranteed for life, and you would need a capital sum of only £83,000 to provide £10,000 a year.

The first method, preserving capital, is what most people do with their own capital. They aim to live off the income and at least keep the capital intact, and preferably increase it. Pension plans, though, have historically been based on the second method, converting the capital accumulated from savings into an income through the purchase of an annuity. But in recent years there have been moves to apply the first method to pension plans so, as we will see, both methods can be used.

How Much Do You Need to Save?

For the moment, we will use the second method to create a rough-and-ready formula for working out how much you need to save. The steps are as follows:

1 Calculate 75% of your current gross earnings.
2 Deduct from this figure £3,000 to allow for the State's pension payments.
3 Now apply the percentage of earnings you expect to get from a defined benefit pension scheme to your current earnings, and deduct the resultant figure from the result of the sum from step 2.
4 Multiply the result of step 3 by the relevant factor from Table 10 (see page 51). This is the capital sum you need in pension funds to meet your retirement income target.
5 Multiply the current value of your account with any defined contribution scheme or personal pension plan by the relevant factor from Table 9 (see page 50). Deduct the resultant figure from the result of step 4. This is the amount you need to accumulate over the period up to retirement.
6 Using Table 9, work out how much you need to save each month over the period up to your intended retirement in order to achieve the figure you arrived at in step 5.

7 Deduct from this monthly savings figure the combined monthly contribution of yourself and your employer to any defined contribution pension scheme, or your own personal monthly contribution to any personal pension plan.

Even if you have pension rights of more than one type, the formula will give you an approximate figure for the amount you need to save. Table 8 gives two examples of how these calculations might operate in practice.

Table 8: How to calculate how much you need to save

Example (1)

John is aged 40 and earns £17,000 a year. He is in a defined benefit scheme and expects to get fifteen-sixtieths (one quarter) of his salary in pension from it. He expects to retire at 60.

1. £17,000 × 75% = £12,750
2. £12,750 − £3,000 = £9,750
3. £9,750 − (£17,000 × 25% =) £4,250 = £5,500
4. £5,500 × 15 = £82,500
5. Does not apply
6. £82,500 ÷ £40,750 = £202 per month
7. Does not apply

Example (2)

Ellen is aged 45 and earns £20,000 a year. She is in a defined contribution scheme where she contributes 5% and her employer contributes 8% of her salary. There is currently £18,000 in her account. She plans to retire at 60.

1. £20,000 × 75% = £15,000
2. £15,000 − £3,000 = £12,000
3. Does not apply
4. £12,000 × 15 = £180,000
5. £180,000 − (£18,000 × 2.08 =) £37,440 = £142,560
6. £142,560 ÷ £26,590 = £536
7. £536 − (£20,000 ÷ 12 × 13% =) £217 = £319 per month

This rough-and-ready formula requires a few warnings. It may understate the value of the State's pensions, and thus overstate your savings needs – although you would be unwise to bet on this. The 5% annual real rate of return may not be achieved. The formula also assumes continued future membership of your current pension scheme. In any event, the saving requirement it throws up is related to your current earnings: as these increase, you will need to increase your savings by the same percentage if you want to reach a target of 75% of your new earnings.

Table 9: Calculating real returns at 5% a year

	Capital sum accumulated from a monthly saving of £100 at a real annual rate of return of 5%	*Escalation factor for current value of pension accounts*
END OF YEAR		
5	£6,810	1.28
7	£10,030	1.41
10	£15,500	1.63
13	£21,830	1.88
15	£26,590	2.08
17	£31,840	2.29
20	£40,750	2.65
25	£58,810	3.39
30	£81,870	4.32

Personal and Occupational Pension Plans

Successive governments have recognized the value of encouraging private pension provision. During the collectivist 1960s and 1970s occupational pension funds were most highly favoured but since the mid-1980s the emphasis has switched to individual provision.

All pension funds that meet the Inland Revenue's criteria share the same set of very favourable tax advantages. They pay no tax on their income or capital gains, so that within a pension fund, money accumulates completely tax-free. Both occupational schemes and personal pension plans allow individuals to take part of the fund as a tax-free cash sum on retirement. But the biggest concession – one that is exclusive to pension funds – is that contributions are, within qualifying limits, fully tax-deductible.

Table 10: Multiplication factor for pension savings

The amount of capital you need to accumulate in a pension fund in order to generate a certain level of income will depend on two factors: your age at retirement and the type of annuity you buy. If you want your income to increase in retirement, you will need to buy an escalating annuity and this will require a larger capital sum. The younger you are when you retire, the larger the capital sum needed for any given level of income.

Minimum multiplication factor *(Use this if you plan to retire at 60 or 65* *and take a level income)*	10
Maximum multiplication factor *(Use this if you plan to retire at 55 or 60* *and want an escalating income)*	20
Average multiplication factor *(Use this if you are uncertain which will apply)*	15

Tax-deductibility gives pension plans a big advantage over other forms of saving. Look at it first from the standard-rate taxpayer's viewpoint. If you put £100 into a tax-exempt plan like a Personal Equity Plan (PEP), £100 is invested. With a pension plan, invest £100 and the Inland Revenue adds another £31.60 (assuming you pay tax at the standard rate), representing a rebate of the income tax you paid on the gross income of £131.60. Actually, the mechanics of getting the tax relief vary – sometimes you pay in the gross amount and get the tax rebate afterwards – but the effect is the same. The net cost to you of putting £1 into a pension plan is 76p if you pay tax at the standard rate and 60p if you pay tax at the higher rate.

Clearly, pension plans give you more bang for your buck than any other form of saving. Other things (such as charges and the rate of return – topics we'll return to in Chapter 10, page 132) being equal, you should end up with a bigger lump sum by saving £100 a month in a pension plan than in a plan that doesn't offer tax-deductibility of contributions. Indeed, if you assume the same rate of return for a tax-exempt PEP and a personal pension plan, and the same charges, a standard-rate taxpayer will end up with a pension fund that is 31.6% larger while a higher-rate taxpayer will end up with one 50% larger than the PEP fund.

Given this huge advantage over rival plans, why doesn't everyone put all their spare savings into pensions plans? There are a good many reasons for this, the most important being:

- There are limits to how much you are allowed to contribute.
- Pension plans are long-term, often inflexible and can involve high charges.
- You cannot draw any cash from a pension plan until you retire.
- All the pension income you draw from a pension plan is subject to income tax.

The contribution limits are generous. Self-employed people rarely run up against these limits, but employees facing a big pension shortfall may find their savings needs are greater than the amounts they are allowed to contribute. Very high earners, too, are constrained by the £82,200 a year ceiling on earnings in relation to which tax relief is given on pension contributions.

Traditional defined benefit occupational schemes were certainly designed for the long-serving employee, and though the lot of the job mover has improved, such plans still favour two categories of people: those who stay with the same employer for 30 years, and the top-earning directors, who can earn a full two-thirds-of-salary pension based on only 20 years' contributions. Lesser mortals, who need 40 years to accumulate a two-thirds pension, may well suspect that one of the reasons why such old-fashioned defined benefits plans persist is that the top managers get far more benefit out of them than the majority of mere employees.

Personal pension plans, introduced in 1986, can be flexible, but much depends on the precise terms the scheme promoter writes into the rules. In particular, high charges can be levied if the plan is discontinued.

You cannot draw cash from a pension plan before you retire. Occupational schemes and personal pension schemes normally set the earliest possible retirement age at 50. Only in very rare cases can you retire before the age of 50. Convincing evidence of ill health must be presented, except for a few special categories of sportsmen and -women and other unusual occupations where the Inland Revenue recognizes that professional careers can end much earlier.

When you do retire, all the accumulated cash, apart from what you withdraw as a tax-free lump sum, must be converted into pension income and this income is all subject to tax. There are ways of avoiding the immediate conversion of the capital into income, but these will only be suitable in a minority of cases. So pension plans' big advantages in terms of tax concessions are balanced by some inflexibilities. But they are bound to play a part in most people's retirement savings.

The intricacies of occupational pension schemes are beyond the scope of this book. But in response to the question: Should you join your employer's occupational pension scheme? the answer is almost certain to be 'Yes'. The reason is simple. Ask how much you have to contribute to the scheme and how much the employer will contribute. Typically the employer will be contributing at least two or three times as much as you are and cannot directly claw back any of those contributions. Even if you 'lose' some of the benefits of a defined benefit scheme through job moves, you will still end up, through your period of membership, with pension rights greater (often far greater) in value than you could have acquired with your own personal contributions to the scheme. As for defined contribution schemes, if the employer is making a contribution, a refusal to join the scheme is equivalent to setting fire to a large bundle of banknotes.

So for the rest of this chapter we will assume either that you are a member of an occupational pension scheme, or that you are working for an employer who does not run such a scheme, or that you are self-employed.

Pension plans for employees

Employees who are members of an occupational pension scheme often face a retirement income shortfall: they may only have a few years' membership of the scheme; they may have worked for several years previously for employers who did not run pension schemes; more important, they may want to create additional funds so that they can retire earlier than normal without suffering too large a reduction in pension.

The one variety of pension plan open to employees in this situation is the Additional Voluntary Contribution plan. Many employers offer such plans alongside their main pension schemes, and there are also free standing AVC plans offered by many financial companies. The rules are the same in both cases: contributions are tax-deductible; the savings accumulate tax-free; and, at retirement, all the cash must be used to buy additional pension income for life – you cannot take any of it as tax-free cash. Only the employee is permitted to contribute to AVC plans.

Employees can contribute up to 15% of their 'pensionable earnings' to pension plans. 'Pensionable earnings' often include the value of any 'perks' on which National Insurance is assessed, and may include any bonuses as well as basic salary. This 15% limit includes any contributions you make to the main occupational scheme. So if you were making contributions of 4% to the main scheme, you could make further contributions of 11% of your earnings to an AVC.

Contributions to AVCs are made net of tax at 25%. So if your salary was £20,000 and you could contribute 11%, you would actually contribute £2,200 − (2,200 × 24% =) £528 = £1,672. If you were a higher-rate taxpayer, you would make net contributions of £1,320 to a company AVC, but with a free standing AVC you would pay £1,672 and would get a rebate of the extra 16% tax through a reduction in your tax bill at the end of the financial year.

Company AVC schemes are normally deposit-based or 'with-profits'. Deposit-based schemes fall into the low-risk category and are suitable for short periods of saving but are far from ideal for terms over five years, so if this is all your company offers, there is a strong case for considering a free standing AVC. With-profits funds are on the borderline between low risk and moderate risk. They invest in a mixture of shares, fixed interest and other investments and grow steadily through the addition of bonuses. They can be a suitable medium for longer-term savings, but the evidence is that over 15 to 25 years you are almost certain to end up with a bigger return from a higher-risk unit-linked Equity fund offered in most free standing AVCs.

Other factors to consider in choosing an AVC are flexibility and charges. Many schemes permit you to vary contributions and make occasional lump sum payments. A few company schemes may be less flexible and permit only a fixed monthly contribution. All AVCs now permit a transfer into a personal pension, but check if there is a charge for this. In general, the charges levied by company AVCs are lower than those of free standing plans. But if you are aiming for maximum growth it may be worth paying a little more in charges to have access to a range of unit-linked equity funds offering the prospect of higher returns.

Although you may not take any tax-free cash from an AVC when you retire, having an AVC will entitle you to a little more tax-free cash from your occupational scheme. This is because in assessing how much tax-free cash you are entitled to, the Inland Revenue looks at the combined value of the main scheme and the AVC.

Since the advent of PEPs financial planners have also started to consider these for pension top-ups. The pros and cons are set out in Table 11.

Table 11: AVC versus PEP for pension top-up

	AVC	PEP
Contributions are tax-deductible	Yes	No
Income in retirement is exempt from tax	No	Yes
Capital is converted into income	Yes	No
You retain ownership of capital	No	Yes

Assuming that you pay tax at 24% and expect to do so in retirement, the tax-deductibility of pension plan contributions means you will end up – assuming the same rate of return and the same charges – with a third more in an AVC fund than a PEP after any given period of savings. But when that capital in the AVC is converted into income, it all bears tax at 24%, whereas you can draw income from the PEP tax-free. Depending on the annuity rate at which you expect to convert AVC capital into income, this results in the net income from the AVC coming out between 5% and 15% ahead of the PEP. But with the PEP, you also retain control of the capital and have tax-free access to it at any time. This makes the PEP look like the winner, but there are three big caveats: most PEPs are much higher-risk and are only suitable for longer terms of saving; a rise in interest rates could mean the AVC fund can be turned into a larger income; and if you pay tax at 40% now but expect to pay tax at only 24% in retirement, then the AVC will generate about 20–25% more income than the PEP.

Few financial planners will opt decisively for one or other option. Which is more suitable will depend on your circumstances and attitude to risk. In general, if you do not like risk, or are very short of pension income, then the greater security of a with-profit AVC fund is probably more desirable. If you have longer to go to retirement, or already have a good basis of pension income, then the chance to retain ownership of your capital may make the PEP more attractive.

Plans for those who are not members of occupational schemes

Anyone who earns enough money to pay tax but is not a member of an occupational pension scheme is allowed to contribute to a different type of plan – a personal pension plan. The two main categories of people this includes are the self-employed and employees whose employers have not set up an occupational scheme.

Personal pension plans have the same tax concessions as other pension schemes, but some of the rules are different. In particular, the amounts you are allowed to contribute are much higher, as shown in Table 12: if you do not have an employer making contributions on your behalf, you need to save more yourself. Again the contributions are fully tax-deductible, thus reducing the net cost of a £100 contribution to £76 for a standard-rate taxpayer and to £60 for a higher-rate taxpayer.

Table 12: Maximum contribution limits to personal pension plans for employees and the self-employed

Age	Percentage of earnings
Under 36	17.5%
36–45	20%
46–50	25%
51–55	30%
56–60	35%
61 or over	40%

The other big difference is that you are allowed to go back in time for six years. Your allowances, in terms of maximum contributions, are carried forward for six years if they are not used at the time. So if you made no contributions for six years you could then make a contribution that used up your allowance for all those years. Such a contribution might be quite large: in fact it might be larger than your taxable income for the tax year in which you pay it – in which case there would be no point, because once you have eliminated your taxable income by deducting a large pension contribution from it, then you cannot save any more tax because you will not pay any. However, this is not a complete bar to making big contributions and getting tax relief on them, because you are also allowed to 'carry back' a contribution to your personal pension plan to the previous tax year, which gives more scope for using the previous six years' allowance effectively.

These rules sound rather complicated and can lead to cold-towel-round-the-head calculations, so let's consider a simple example:

Andrew has unused allowances for pension contributions from the previous six years of £15,000. He has inherited a lump sum of £30,000 and would like to add £15,000 to his existing personal pension plan. But in the current tax year he only has taxable income of £10,000. So this is the maximum it makes sense to contribute for this year. However, in the previous year he had taxable income of £8,000, so he can still make one lump sum payment of £15,000 into his plan, and offset £10,000 against the current year's tax liability and £5,000 against the preceding year's. This means he will get an immediate refund of the tax he paid in the previous year on £5,000 of income, and a reduction in the tax bill due to be paid on the current year's income.

As in this example, if you are self-employed, you will make contributions gross and then claim either a tax rebate from the Inland Revenue or a reduction in your next tax bill. Most employees, on the other hand, will make regular contributions net of standard-rate tax. Additional tax relief for higher-rate taxpayers will normally be made through a year-end adjustment. Employees' one-off lump sum contributions will normally be made gross, with tax relief provided as a tax rebate.

All personal pension plans are of the defined contribution type: you save money, it accumulates in your own personal account and at retirement the capital is used to buy you a lifetime pension income. Retirement can be at any time between the ages of 50 and 75, but you do not have to retire in a real sense to start drawing a pension. In fact, if you have several plans you can be drawing a pension from one while still contributing to another. So long as you have earned income, you're entitled to go on contributing right up to the age of 75. This means that such plans benefit the self-employed, who may well choose to retire gradually.

At retirement, when you convert the capital in the fund into income, you can draw out 25% of the fund as a tax-free cash sum; the rest has to be used to buy a lifetime pension income. But you may also defer converting the fund into income through the purchase of an annuity. This might be an advantage if, for example, you wanted to take some income to supplement your earnings but did not want to retire completely; or if interest rates were low at the time, since this would mean converting your capital into income at a disadvantageous rate. Exactly this happened to people with personal pension plans in 1993 when interest rates fell sharply. The same sum of money in a personal pension plan in 1993 would have purchased a lifetime income of 25% less than that it could have bought in 1992. Deferment is therefore a valuable option.

If you do defer conversion of your fund into an annuity, you must still draw some income. The minimum is 35% of the income you would have been entitled to draw, and this income will be subject to income tax. The capital in your fund can be invested as you choose, so there is scope for capital growth, and if you die before it is finally converted into an annuity (the latest date for this is age 75), then your inheritors may receive the balance of your fund after deduction of a 35% tax charge.

Personal pension plans usually offer you a multiple choice menu of investments. The main categories are:

- **Cash deposit funds.** You might want to use one of these if you put money into your plan very close to your intended retirement date. Or you might want to switch your money from more risky funds to a cash deposit fund in the year or two before retirement.

- **With-profits funds.** These invest in a mixture of shares and other assets and allocate the returns to your account in the form of bonuses. Usually the regular annual bonuses are at a fairly low level and a large part of the return, often as much as half, will come from the 'terminal' bonuses credited when you retire. These funds appear less risky than unitized funds, but do not be misled by apparently modest changes in bonus rates. A reduction of, say, 1% in regular bonus could cut many thousands off your final fund. Likewise, there could be a reduction in terminal bonus in response to a fall in the stock market just before you retire.

- **Fixed interest funds.** These unitized funds are halfway between the safety of cash and the riskier equity funds. They can be a good choice when interest rates are high because when you pay no tax on the interest – which is always the case with pension funds – the rate of return can be good.

- **Managed funds.** These unitized funds invest in a similar range of investments as with-profit funds but without the bonus system. Their wide range of investments should make them less risky than equity funds, but you need to look at the actual record of individual funds to see if this is the case.

- **Moderate-risk equity funds**, including funds investing in large UK companies and funds investing in a spread of shares in the world's major stock markets. These are generalist funds which aim to spread risk widely and invest in a fairly cautious way. In the short term they are riskier than with-profit funds but in the long term (15 years or more) have usually produced larger payouts.

- **Higher-risk equity funds.** This includes many varieties of specialist funds, for example funds investing only in shares in Japan, or America, or Emerging Markets, or technology-related companies. You need to be careful in choosing these since they can produce spectacularly good or very bad returns over periods of up to five years.

Some results of investing in these funds are shown in Table 13. These show a wide variation. Over 10 years or more, equity funds usually outpace cash, fixed interest, and managed funds. Usually, over a 15-year period, UK equity funds also outpace with-profits funds. Over a 10-year period, with-profits funds normally come out ahead over periods ending when the stock market is low, while equity funds usually win over periods ending when the market is at a high level. The pattern of returns from more specialist funds is less predictable. For example, funds investing in Japan were among the very best performers in the 1980s, but few investment managers would expect the Japanese stock market ever again to produce the spectacularly high returns it generated in that decade.

Table 13: Results of investment in personal pension plans

Fund accumulated by monthly contribution of £200. Payout figures for average fund in each sector. All figures to 1 July 1995. (See also Table 18 on page 136.)

Type of fund	*Period of saving (years)*		
	5	10	15
Cash deposit	£12,596	£33,703	£68,530
With-profits	£14,060	£45,225	£123,756
Managed	£14,332	£36,546	£86,920
Fixed interest	£13,495	£36,269	£74,114
UK equity	£14,166	£36,988	£97,887
International equity	£14,526	£35,957	£86,992
Far Eastern equity	£15,281	£37,835	N/A
North American equity	£15,338	£38,642	N/A

Source: Money Management Personal Pensions Survey, October 1995

With most plans, you may contribute to several funds simultaneously, and you may also switch your money from one fund to another. So you can change the risk profile of your plan as time goes on. You could start, say, 20 years away from retirement with all your savings in equity funds, and switch part to with-profits 10 years from retirement, switch some more into fixed interest five years from retirement and switch the lot to a cash deposit fund for the last year or two if the outlook for the financial markets looked uncertain. A few pension plan providers build this type of reducing risk profile into their plans so that it is done for you automatically.

Another useful feature of many plans is the 'multiple policy'. When you contribute, say, £500 per month you do not get one plan but 50 plans. In reality, they are only computer numbers, but this allows you to treat each of the 50 segments separately. This makes retiring in stages even easier, allowing you to convert your capital into income in steps, say at age 60, 63 and 66, instead of all at once. But you could also do this on an annual basis, deciding each year how many segments to convert into pension income.

The sophisticated name for this is 'phased retirement'. An adviser with a phased retirement computer program can tell you how many segments you will need to encash each year to achieve any given income target. Because each time you encash a segment, you take 25% of the fund as tax-free cash, much of this income will be tax-free. Moreover, since your money remains invested in funds and – hopefully – goes on growing in value, you should get more out of your fund than if you converted it all into income in year one of retirement. A final benefit of a phased retirement programme is that if you die before the age of 75, the money remaining in the pension funds can go to your inheritors free of all taxes; if you convert all your fund into income early in retirement, then the capital is gone and the pension income dies with you.

These aspects of phased retirement sound attractive, but you need quite a large fund – at least £100,000 – for it to work. And it does involve taking some risk, since your money stays invested, though you can contain this by using low-risk funds.

You do not have to choose a specific type of plan at the outset to be able to use phased retirement. You can wait until just before you retire, at which point you simply take the funds you have accumulated in different pension plans and transfer them all into one personal pension plan that provides the needed segmentation and a suitable range of investment funds.

Phased retirement is one way of deferring the conversion of your accumulated capital into income through the purchase of an annuity. But the 1994 budget introduced another method – deferment – which applies to any personal pension plan. This allows you to defer the conversion of the fund into income up to the age of 75. Again, you could be exposed to risk here: if you kept your plan invested in a high-risk equity fund which fell in value, the eventual conversion of the fund into an annuity would produce a lower income than it would have several years earlier. But plan providers also offer low-risk funds where you can be sure that your capital will remain intact even after withdrawing the minimum level of income.

The annuity options

When you convert your capital into income through the purchase of an annuity, you do not have to buy the annuity from your pension plan company. You can 'shop the market' for the best rate – or, more realistically, get an adviser to do this for you. This is well worth while because at any one time there is usually a difference of at least 15% – and often more – between the best and worst annuity rates offered by different insurance companies. So you could increase your lifetime pension income by 15% or more by getting the best available deal.

The main restriction on the kind of annuity you can buy is that it must provide an income for the rest of your life. But there are options: for instance, the income can continue at a lower rate for the life of your spouse if he or she survives you, and you can have a level income or an income that increases at a set rate of, say, 2% each year. Both these options reduce the initial amount of income you get from a given amount of capital.

Married people often purchase annuities that continue during the surviving partner's life. But depending on your ages, you may achieve the same result by taking an income only for your own life, using part of the extra income you get from this annuity (as compared with what you would have got from one that also paid out during your spouse's life) to pay premiums on a whole of life insurance policy for the benefit of your spouse. If you die first, your spouse uses the payout from this policy to buy a separate annuity. The taxation of life annuities is different from pension annuities: all the income from a pension annuity is taxed whereas a large part of the income payments from a life annuity are regarded as a return of capital and are therefore not taxed at all. So this method may produce a higher income for your spouse.

Annuity rates depend on the yield currently available on Government securities or gilts, since insurance companies invest capital mainly in gilts to secure the annuity income payments. This yield level in turn is affected by many factors (see Chapter 5, pages 77–79), in particular the current and expected future rate of inflation, the level of short-term interest rates and the behaviour of the Sterling exchange rate. The level of annuity rates can change by 15% or more within a year, so the timing of your purchase is important. Certainly you should not automatically convert your accumulated fund into income just because you happen to have reached your 60th or 65th birthday.

Investing lump sums in pension plans

Given their right to carry forward six years' contribution allowances, many people will find that their contribution entitlements will far exceed the sums they can afford to save out of income, even allowing for the tax-deductibility of contributions. But there is no rule that the contributions have to come from your earned income: it can often make sense to invest lump sums of capital in your pension plan. So if you are eligible to contribute to a personal pension and inherit or otherwise acquire a capital sum, it is always worth considering using some of it as a pension top-up.

An interesting phenomenon concerning the effects of tax-deductibility is worth a closer look since it provides good opportunities to earn a very high rate of return on capital. So long as you are a standard-rate taxpayer, the enhancement rate – the amount by which tax-deductibility increases your net contribution to a pension plan – is 31.6%. But the effect of this on the annual return you earn on the investment varies with time. The shorter the period, the more the tax-deductibility of contributions increases the annual rate of return. So there is useful scope for eleventh-hour pension plan investments, as this example shows:

Martin is aged 60, self-employed and intending to retire next year. He has taxable income of £20,000 for the current year in excess of his normal pension plan contribution, and has unused contribution allowances carried forward from the past six years of £20,000. If he makes a lump sum contribution of £20,000, it will eliminate a £4,800 tax bill, so the net cost will be £15,200. Next year, when he retires, he will be able to take a quarter of the pension fund back as tax-free cash, so he will get £5,000 back and have £15,000 in the fund. At that point the net cost, after the tax saving and cash withdrawal, of having £15,000 in the fund will be £10,200 – which means he will have made a return of almost 50% in one year, or slightly less allowing for the timing of the cash withdrawal.

Making your own investment decisions

If you want the ultimate tax-exempt investment fund, where you have complete control over the investments within the fund, then a Self Invested Personal Pension scheme (SIPP) may appeal. The SIPP has the normal personal pension qualification and contribution rules, and the same tax treatment. But it gives you almost complete control over the investments, because you can choose these yourself.

A few investments are, it is true, not permitted within a SIPP, among them residential property and commodity futures. But shares (lised on the London or other world stock markets), commercial property or unitized property funds, investment trusts, unit trusts, offshore funds, most types of fixed interest security and of course cash deposits are all allowed. A SIPP can also be used to implement a phased retirement programme.

SIPPs are designed more for lump sum investment than for regular contributions. Their charges tend to be flat-rate, and running this type of plan with small contributions is simply not viable. But if you want to run your pension fund in the same way as your other investments, it is well worth considering. Also, if you have a transfer value in a previous pension scheme and want to have a wider choice of investments – and lower charges – then apply with many insurance company plans, then transferring your former pension rights to a SIPP may be attractive.

5 ‖ Tax-free Savings with Low Risk

Most people will want to have some of their savings in plans where the risk of any loss is low. In fact, if you intend to use the money within the next five years, you should certainly keep some of your money in the plans described in this chapter. Over this sort of period, there is no knowing whether the stock market will produce gains or losses, so unless you can hold on for the longer haul, you could lose money when you cash in an equity savings plan. Rather than go all out for the maximum return, therefore, you would do better to have a lower but more secure return with little or no chance of loss.

Tax-free Deposits

TESSAs

The only tax-exempt plan in the UK that is a simple deposit is the Tax Exempt Special Savings Account or TESSA. TESSA has become Britain's most popular tax shelter since the scheme was launched in 1991.

The interest on money in a TESSA is free of income tax, both during its term and when it is withdrawn, but this depends on your leaving your money in the scheme until the fifth anniversary of opening it. If you draw out any of the capital you contributed to the account within this five-year period, all the interest will become taxable. At the end of the five years you can draw out all the interest and capital. Alternatively, you can transfer up to £9,000 into a new TESSA for the following five years.

The maximum you may invest in a TESSA is £9,000 over a five-year term. The maximum amount in the first year is £3,000, followed by £1,800 in subsequent years. If you start off with a £3,000 deposit, you can then invest £1,800 in years two to four and £600 in the fifth year; or you may invest a flat £1,800 a year. If you are transferring from a maturing TESSA to a new one, you may invest an initial £9,000 but may not add to the account during its five-year term.

You may withdraw some interest from the account during the term: the maximum is the equivalent of the gross interest that has been credited, minus the 20% tax that would normally be deducted from a taxable account. So if the gross rate of interest being credited to your account was 7%, the maximum you could withdraw would be 5.6%.

Table 14 compares figures for the amount that you would accumulate over five years at an interest rate of 8% gross with the figures for an account where you paid tax at 20%. The higher the interest rate you get, the more valuable the exemption from income tax. Perhaps fewer TESSAs would have been opened if interest rates in 1991 had not been over 10%.

Table 14: Tax-free interest in a TESSA

Year	Amount invested during year	Year-end value of TESSA earning 8% gross CAR	Year-end value of taxable account earning 6.4% net CAR
1	£3,000	£3,240	£3,192
2	£1,800	£5,443	£5,311
3	£1,800	£7,822	£7,567
4	£1,800	£10,392	£9,966
5	£600	£11,871	£11,243
Total invested	£9,000		
Annual interest from year 6 onwards		£950	£719

You can close a TESSA at any time before the fifth anniversary. All the interest will be taxable, but – apart from any termination charge made by the firm providing the account – there are no other penalties.

The vast majority of TESSAs are operated by banks and building societies. Most of them pay variable interest, and – as with standard accounts – interest is usually credited six-monthly. Many bank and building society TESSAs allow you to start with as little as £1, but some schemes paying higher interest require you to invest the maximum in each year. A few offer still higher interest, but only if you deposit enough in a taxable account to transfer the full £9,000 into a TESSA over the five-year period.

In theory, you can transfer your TESSA from one bank or building society to another. You might want to do this if the interest paid to you was cut to an uncompetitive level. The terms of the scheme require TESSA operators to permit you to make a transfer, which will usually entail a relatively modest charge of up to £25. But many TESSA operators refuse to accept transfers from an existing account because the Inland Revenue requires them to make an extensive check on records.

The vast majority of TESSAs pay a variable rate of interest. Usually this is in line with the gross rate being paid on higher-interest accounts that require a larger deposit than the TESSA. A few TESSA operators offer fixed-rate accounts. Some will fix the interest rate for a year at a time – so that you have the option each year of having a fixed or a variable rate – while others offer a fixed rate for the full five years. Clearly it makes sense to secure a five-year fixed rate only if interest rates are at a relatively high level and the general expectation is that they will fall. When interest rates look likely to rise, a variable rate is preferable.

If you are saving money for a five-year period, TESSA is a simple, low-risk way to do so. The returns are likely to be lower than from riskier types of savings, but the fact that you have access to your money within the five years if you need it is a very important consideration if your circumstances change.

Looking at this from another point of view, so long as you are a taxpayer you have little to lose by starting a TESSA. Even if you do need your capital earlier than the fifth anniversary, the only penalty you will suffer is payment of the tax that would have been due if you had left the money in an ordinary taxable account.

The same argument applies to older people who often think they cannot plan five years ahead and say that they may not even last that long: but if you are going to die, you might as well die with the money in a tax-exempt rather than a taxable account. No tax is payable if a TESSA is closed early on death.

Verdict: TESSA may not be the most glamorous tax-free savings plan, but it is secure and offers a worthwhile tax saving. Since most people need reliable short-term savings schemes, TESSA is likely to have a part to play in your plans.

Better than the Lottery

One rather odd tax-exempt investment gives you the chance of winning a million pounds as well as a reasonable return on your money. This is Premium Bonds, an unusual lottery run by the Department for National Savings. What is unusual about it is that you never lose your stake – you can encash your bonds and get your money back at any time. Because of the structure of the prize draw, if you invest £10,000 or more you can be pretty confident of getting a regular tax-free return of around 5%.

The way Premium Bonds work is that a percentage of the total amount invested in bonds is allocated as prize money. The rate of interest is usually comparable with the rates of interest paid on building society accounts. This, in effect, is the rate of annual interest the Government is paying you to borrow your money.

The vast majority of the prize money is handed out in £50 prizes: there are so many, in fact, that the odds of winning a £50 prize from any £1 Premium Bond in any monthly draw are quite good: around 1 in 16,000. The chance of winning the top £1 million prize with a £1 bond in any monthly draw is rather less hopeful: 1 in 5,000,000,000, so even holding the maximum £20,000 investment in Premium Bonds is unlikely to make you a millionaire: it just improves the odds to 1 in 260,000 or so.

But that is not the point. The point is that if you do hold £10,000 or £20,000 in bonds, the random draw of numbers each month means that over a year, you are likely to collect sufficient £50 prizes to give you a return of about 5% on your money. Of course there will be months when you get no prizes – and there may even be several such months in a row – but over time the prizes are likely to average out at the same rate as the rate that prize money represents of the whole fund.

The larger the number of bonds you hold (up to the £20,000 maximum), the more likely you are to get a reasonably regular flow of prizes. The National Savings statistics show that with £10,000 in bonds, the odds are almost even on collecting a prize in any draw, while if you have £20,000 in bonds, the likelihood of a prize in any draw rises to nearly 74%.

Premium Bonds have long been a favourite stocking-filler for youngsters, but more recently the attraction of a regular tax-exempt 5% plus the chance of a big prize (there are £100,000, £50,000 and £25,000 prizes each month as well as the £1 million) has encouraged more adults to place larger sums in bonds. It certainly compares extremely well with the National Lottery.

Verdict: Premium bonds can be considered an investment if you invest enough (over £5,000) to be sure of getting a steady flow of small prizes. That and the chance of a big prize make them a much more interesting type of investment than a (taxable) building society account.

Offshore deposits can be tax-free

Your own tax position may enable you to make use of certain offshore deposit funds to earn tax-free interest. The funds, often called 'money funds', place money on deposit with major banks. Usually such funds come in two forms, a Distributor and an Accumulator. With the Distributor, all the interest is paid out, usually at half-yearly intervals. The interest is paid gross but is subject to UK income tax, so Distributor funds offer no scope for tax saving. But with the Accumulator version, all the interest is accumulated and adds to the price of shares in the fund. When you sell shares, all the profit is taxable as income if you are a UK resident.

This allows for a lengthy deferment of tax, because the profit element in the price of shares is low in the early years of such an investment. For example, assume you invest £10,000 in an Accumulator fund that earns interest at 8% gross. The shares are priced at 100p when you buy them and at the end of the year are worth 108p. At the end of the first year, you want to encash enough shares to provide a 6% net income. You encash 564 shares at 108p providing you with £609.12. Of this, only the profit element (8p on every share) is taxable, so only £45.12 will be assessed to tax at 20%. The tax payable will be £9.02 and you will have your required net income.

The tax liability is not eliminated, only deferred. Each year, the interest or profit will represent a higher proportion of the price of each share, so the taxable proportion of the amount you get from each disposal of shares will rise. But in the meantime, you earn interest on the gross interest that is accumulated in the fund, and will therefore earn a higher return, even after paying all the tax, than you would have earned by investing in taxable UK deposits.

But your own tax position may enable you to escape tax on the interest completely. For example, you may know that in, say, four years' time you will have a year or two in which you will have no income. If you cash in your offshore Accumulator fund shares during this period, then so long as your total income remains below the personal allowance, you will not be liable to any tax. Women who are currently working but are planning to take a complete break from work while they bring up children are one group who can take advantage of this.

Just because a fund is 'offshore' does not necessarily mean that it is risky. These money funds are based in Jersey or Guernsey, are run by large and reputable UK companies or banks, and the funds themselves place money on deposit only with large and secure banks.

Verdict: Offshore money funds may enable you to avoid paying income tax on your interest. At the very least, they enable you to increase your return by deferring the tax bills. But the exercise is only worthwhile if you have a sizeable sum to invest in this way.

Five-year schemes from National Savings

For the past 25 years National Savings has always had a five-year tax-exempt plan on offer: National Savings Certificates. The interest rate on these (each time it changes there is a new Issue of NSCs) is not always competitive, because National Savings does not change its rates as often as some of its competitors in the financial world. But for the same reason, there are times when NSCs offer an outstanding deal. Being tax-exempt, they do not have to be declared on your tax return either when you make an investment or when you cash it in.

In fact there are two types of National Savings Certificates: the fixed interest and the index-linked. The fixed interest variety offers a tax-exempt interest rate, usually expressed as '$x\%$ a year', but in practice the face value of a certificate grows by a set amount each year. The growth in the early years is low, so if you cash them in during years one or two, you get a poor return, while if you hold them for the full five years, you get the advertised rate for the five-year term.

There is usually a limit to how much you are allowed to invest in NSCs. This has normally been either £5,000 or £10,000 per individual in each issue. In addition to this, you are usually allowed to reinvest a further amount (often up to £10,000) from maturing previous issues of NSCs. And in addition to that, there is a little-known loophole that lets you invest a far greater amount. You are allowed to invest not just on your own behalf but also 'under trust' for children and for your spouse. So, assuming the existence of a current NSC with a £10,000 investment limit, a husband and wife could invest £10,000 each, plus a further £10,000 each under trust for each other, making £40,000, plus a further £10,000 under trust for each of their children aged under 18. These trust rules apply to both the fixed interest and index-linked varieties of NSC.

Because the fixed interest NSC usually offers a competitive net rate for standard-rate taxpayers, it often represents an excellent deal for higher-rate taxpayers. If building society accounts offer 7% net of standard-rate tax, the fixed interest NSC will usually offer a bit more – say 7.5% net. As a higher-rate taxpayer, you would need to get a pre-tax interest rate of 12.5% to end up with 7.5% net – and you would be unlikely to find that on offer anywhere else without a lot of risk attached.

The index-linked NSC was an attractive investment when the inflation rate was high, but is not so attractive if you expect a low rate of inflation in the future. It also requires you to keep your money invested for five years – you can get it out earlier, but you then lose the benefit of index-linking. The value of your capital is increased in line with the Retail Prices Index each month, and on top of that you get a bonus on the fifth anniversary. If you encash early, you get a lower return. In the past few years the effective annualized interest rate from the index-linking and the bonus have been between 5% and 6% a year, making index-linked NSCs rather uncompetitive for standard-rate taxpayers. But for higher-rate taxpayers, the net returns from the Index-Linked Certificates can be more attractive.

If there are signs that inflation is about to accelerate again – such signs could include steep Sterling devaluation, rapidly rising wages, and a boom in property prices – then index-linked NSCs could, as they have in the past, provide a useful defence against inflation for some of your savings.

With both varieties of NSC, the term is five years. If you do nothing at the end of the period, the Department for National Savings will automatically transfer your savings to an account earning the General Extension Rate, which is normally a low, uncompetitive rate of interest.

NSCs are designed for adults but National Savings also has a five-year fixed rate investment specially for children, the Children's Guaranteed Bonus Bond, often referred to as the Children's Bond. It usually offers a very competitive rate that is impossible to beat with security elsewhere, together with complete exemption from tax. The rate is fixed for five years and when a bond matures it can be 'rolled over' into a new one so long as the child is aged 16 or under at that time.

Since children are normally non-taxpayers anyway (see Chapter 2, page 29), you might think there is little merit in a tax-free scheme. But remember the 'parental gift' rules that can penalize interest if parents are the donors of capital. Investment in the Children's Bond defeats this rule and allows parents to give their children capital and earn good interest on it without falling foul of the Inland Revenue. And, unlike bank or building society accounts, a child cannot lay its hands on the money in a Children's Bond until a bond matures and he or she is aged over 16 at the time – which grandparents often find an attractive feature.

The only drawback to the Children's Bond is that there is currently a maximum investment of £1,000 per child.

Verdict: National Savings' fixed interest NSCs and Children's Bonus Bonds can offer attractive interest rates with complete tax exemption. Since you can buy them in small units (usually £25 at a time), they offer a simple way to tuck away money for a five-year term.

Tax-free Income from Bonds

'Bond' is a term that has unfortunately been widely misused in the UK financial world. Though it is used by various financial companies as a name for their products, what it actually means is a fixed interest security quoted on a stock exchange. Bonds are loans that have been turned into securities that can be traded between investors. This makes it easier for borrowers to raise money: investors know they can get access to their capital through a marketplace where bonds are traded.

The amount of bonds in issue is vast and greatly exceeds the value of shares quoted on stock markets. Government debt is one factor: all governments borrow money by issuing bonds, and most governments issue more new bonds than they redeem old ones. Then there are international agencies like the World Bank; local governments and municipalities; and companies.

Bonds can be an attractive investment for people who need income, because they usually pay higher rates of income than either short-term deposits or shares. If that interest is tax-free, you can often get a return well in excess of inflation.

There are many different types of bond but the most common type is where the issuer promises to pay a fixed rate of interest for a set period and undertakes to redeem the bond at its face value at the end of this period. The rate of interest paid (the 'coupon') will be in line with the level prevailing in the market when the bond is issued. Bonds may be issued with lives (the term up to the redemption date) of anything from one to 30 years. In the UK Government bond or gilt market, bonds with remaining lives of under five years are classed as short-dated, those with remaining lives of between five and 15 years are medium-dated, and those with remaining lives of over 15 years are long-dated.

Calculating the return

As a potential investor, you need to know what return you would get from a bond and how this return compares with that from other bonds. This is not as simple as it looks, because though you can buy some bonds at their face value, other bonds may trade in the marketplace for more or less than their face value, so that you would make a capital loss or gain if you held them to redemption. In order to compare all these bonds with each other, we cannot use the simple relationship between the interest the bond pays on its face value (the coupon) and the price you pay for it, because this ignores the effect of any capital gain or loss. So the redemption yield, which is the annualized return to redemption, including any capital gain or loss as well as the interest, is the main comparative measure of value in the bond market.

If interest rates were 10%, a newly issued bond with a 10-year life would pay 10% interest. But what about a 15-year bond issued five years ago when interest rates were 8%, with a coupon of 8%? Clearly nobody will pay its issue price, or 100, for it now, when they could instead buy a newly issued bond with a similar life paying 10%. So the market price of the old bond will have to stand at a level where the capital gain over the remaining life, added to the interest, produces an annual return similar to the 10% offered by the new bond. Suppose the old bond's price fell to 80. Then the interest of 8% on the face value of 100, or 8 per annum, would be equal to a 10% annual interest on the purchase price of 80. But on top of this the investor would make a capital gain of 20 over the next 10 years, because the bond would still be redeemed at its face value of 100. So the price would not fall to 80 but to about 90, a level where the buyer will get an annual return of 10% consisting of about 9% and 1% capital gain.

The same applies to bonds issued when interest rates were higher than they are now. Say interest rates today are 8%, and a 10-year bond newly issued at 100 pays 8% interest. What about a 15-year bond issued five years ago when interest rates were 10%? Investors will pay more for it than its original issue price. They will pay the amount where the annual capital loss over the period to redemption balances out the extra interest received, leaving a combined annual return of 8%. This will be made up of about 9% interest minus 1% capital loss. This will apply at a price of about 110 for a bond with a remaining life of 10 years.

These technicalities are important, because at any one time there are far more bonds around that were issued when interest rates were at levels above or below today's level than there are newly issued bonds, and for a variety of reasons, these bonds may offer you a better deal.

There are two other crucial factors in evaluating bonds: credit risk and volatility.

Credit risk

Credit risk is the risk of a borrower defaulting and either not paying the interest for a while or defaulting on both interest payments and capital repayments. The British Government, it is assumed, cannot default, so gilt-edged securities are regarded as having no credit risk. Then come bonds issued by the UK local authorities. There is no formal Government guarantee behind these bonds, and there has never been a legal case to establish that the Government is actually responsible for these debts, but it is assumed that, if it came to the crunch, no UK Government would let a local authority default on its debts. Still, these bonds tend to offer slightly higher redemption yields than gilts, mainly because it is less easy to buy and sell them in quantity. After the local authorities come companies. Here there is a separate pecking order, starting with the largest and oldest-established companies, the 'blue chips', and moving progressively down through smaller and less financially secure concerns. The higher the perceived credit risk, the higher the yield investors will demand, so in the bond market, 'the higher the yield, the higher the risk' always applies. You can choose to buy only UK Government bonds with no credit risk or to buy riskier bonds and collect higher returns.

Bonds issued by companies bring in another aspect of credit risk. Some bonds are debentures, which are similar to mortgages: the loan is secured against specific assets with a legal deed, so that the company cannot sell or otherwise pledge the assets to anyone else. Other bonds are unsecured. And some bonds are actually in the form of shares – preference shares, which rank for payment of interest and capital only after any other loans the company may have. In boom times, when most companies are making satisfactory profits, these distinctions may not appear to matter much. In a severe recession, when some companies hit the rocks, they are crucial. If you own a debenture you are fairly sure to get something back – very likely a large portion of your capital – even if the company defaults on the interest and goes bust. But if you own an unsecured loan stock or preference share in the same company, you may end up with nothing.

Volatility

Credit risk is one important feature of bond investment. Another is volatility – the tendency of prices to vary on a day-to-day basis.

Suppose we have interest rates at 8%, but some sudden economic upheaval forces interest rates up to 10% overnight. How much will bond prices change? The movement will depend on the bond's coupon and its remaining life. Say we had one bond with an 8% coupon that was due for redemption in a year's time and another, also with an 8% coupon, that had a life of 20 years to redemption. Clearly the price of the bond that is due for redemption next year at 100 cannot fall far below 100. Over a year, you only need a 2% capital gain to add to the 8% coupon to get a 10% return. So the price of this bond might drop from 100 to a little over 98. But the fall in the 20-year bond price must be much larger in order to generate sufficient capital gain to produce an overall return of 10% a year. The price of this bond will therefore fall to about 85.

As this example shows, the prices of long-dated bonds will always move by a larger amount in relation to any given change up or down in the level of interest rates than those of short-dated bonds. Longer-dated bonds are more volatile and are therefore regarded as a riskier investment than short-dated bonds.

How to Buy Bonds Exempt from Tax

The interest from bonds is normally taxable (see Chapter 2, page 18). Escaping tax on the income is what is needed to make bonds a really attractive investment.

Corporate Bond PEPs

The way to avoid income tax on bond interest is to buy bonds through a Personal Equity Plan. Despite the name, the PEP rules were changed in 1995 to permit investment in Sterling bonds issued by UK companies. Gilt-edged stocks are not eligible. The interest received from corporate bonds through PEPs is exempt from income tax, and any capital gains are also tax-free.

Corporate bond PEPs, as they are called, usually offer a managed portfolio of bonds. Obviously it could be risky to own just one or two companies' bonds, so a spread is desirable. But if you are prepared to select your own bonds, you can do so by setting up a self-select PEP (see page 81).

Individuals who are resident for tax purposes in the UK and are aged over 18 may invest up to £6,000 in each fiscal year (6 April to 5 April) in a PEP. You may only invest in one such PEP in any fiscal year, so you cannot spread your money between different plans each year as you can with other types of investment.

As soon as your money is invested in a PEP, you are entitled to withdraw tax-free income. You may also withdraw any or all of your capital at any time without paying any tax. None of your PEP transactions, income or capital, need to be recorded in your tax return. Many plan managers provide plans that permit monthly contributions from £50 per month, so PEPs can be used to accumulate capital too.

More people, though, are likely to use corporate bond PEPs to generate tax-free income from their capital. But it is important not to be seduced by the highest income figure. As explained above, some of the income you get could reduce the future value of your capital. So if the general level of interest rates were 8% it would be quite possible for one plan to offer a 10% income – by buying riskier bonds. Always look for a clear statement of policy from the investment managers on the subject of credit risk or the quality of bonds in which they will invest.

Another important factor is the level of annual charge levied by the managers of such a fund. Some managers have made great play of the expertise required to manage bond funds, but in practice, most bonds once bought are held for long periods, and unlike shares there is usually less need to buy and sell to secure profits or avoid losses. In fact there is no convincing reason why charges on corporate bond PEPs should be higher than on equity PEPs, and many good reasons why they should be lower. A management fee of 1% per annum is the maximum it is reasonable to pay for a fund of this type; there are funds which charge only 0.75%. Nor should you pay a high initial charge on entry to such a fund. The initial charge you pay on entry to an Equity fund, which reduces the capital actually invested, can be made up by capital growth, but the scope for growth in a bond fund is very limited, so any initial charge is likely to represent a permanent erosion of your capital. A 3% initial charge is the maximum you should be prepared to pay.

Few UK investment managers have much experience of managing bond funds, because bonds were such an unpopular investment in the inflationary 1970s and 1980s. So in choosing a plan, you can ignore managers' performance records with their equity investments – the skills required in bond investment are entirely different – and focus simply on whether they have actual experience of managing funds that invest solely in fixed interest investments, and what their track record with these funds has been in the past.

The one type of fixed interest fund most companies have run in the past has been a fund investing in gilt-edged securities, but do not expect many managers to make any reference to this in their sales pitches for corporate bond PEPs. The evidence shows that only a handful of managers have been able to produce a better performance with these funds than you could have achieved for yourself by making random purchases of gilts in the market.

No doubt skill in managing corporate bond funds will develop over time, but there is no reason why you should risk your cash with inexperienced managers.

As with other PEPs, it is possible to select your own investments by setting up a self-select PEP with a stockbroker. Several firms offer plans with no initial charges and no annual management fee, simply charging dealing commissions on purchase and sale and administration charges on collecting dividends. There are some very large companies (British Gas, British Telecom, and BAT, for example) which have suitable bonds, so you can minimize risk by investing only in bonds issued by companies of this type.

Corporate bond PEPs were introduced only in mid-1995 and doubtless there will be improvements in the plans on offer as managers get to grips with the technicalities. The important things to remember are that a higher yield must carry a higher risk, that the quality of bonds in a fund is important to avoid the risk of capital loss and that high charges can eat into both your capital and your income.

Verdict: Corporate bond PEPs provide a high tax-exempt income which many retired investors want. Scope for capital growth is minimal, but these plans can still play a very useful part in retirement savings. But take care to avoid plans with high charges; pick ones where the managers have demonstrable skill and experience in managing fixed interest investments.

How to Get Tax-free Returns from Bonds

Interest from UK bonds is taxable. But capital gains, even if they are taxable, can escape tax if you make careful use of your annual capital gains tax exemption. There is one category of bond that allows you to do just this and secure high tax-free returns over periods from one to 10 years.

Zeros

The bonds in question are Zero Dividend Preference Shares in split-capital investment trusts, and since these usually offer redemption yields about 1% higher than those from gilt-edged, the tax-free returns can be considerably higher than from taxable investments.

Split-capital investment trusts have two or more types of share.

Money is raised from the shareholders and invested in one pool. One type of shares may get the capital, another type may get the income. Zero Dividend Preference Shares (or Zeros) are usually combined with Ordinary Income shares in a split-capital trust. Though they are called shares, the Zero Dividend Preference Shares actually get a fixed annual rate of capital growth, all of which is paid in the form of a capital gain at redemption, so in reality they are bonds. The Ordinary Income shares get all the rest of the income and capital from the investments of the trust. The capital gain on Zeros is potentially taxable, but individuals will often not actually be liable to the tax.

The Zeros provide gearing for the other shareholders in a split-capital trust. The capital they subscribe will create larger returns for the other shareholders – but also more risk. For the Zeros, though, the risk is limited and depends on the original capital structure of the trust, which determines the degree of cover. Cover for Zeros defines the extent to which the current value of the trust's assets exceeds the total amount needed to pay out the Zeros at redemption. So if the total value of a trust's Zeros at redemption is £30 million and cover is 1.5, it means the trust has £45 million in assets. The Zeros have first claim on all assets at the redemption date, so until they are paid off the other shareholders get nothing.

Every split capital trust has a redemption date at which all the trust's assets will be sold and the proceeds paid out to the different classes of shareholder. This means it is easy to value Zeros. In practice, the life of a trust may be extended, but there will then be an opportunity for Zero shareholders to sell at the original redemption price.

The redemption yield on different Zeros varies in line with cover. If cover is less than 1, so that the trust has less assets now than it needs to pay off the Zeros, the yield will be higher than if cover is, say, 1.8. But if there are still many years to go until redemption, it is reasonable to assume some growth in the value of the trust's investments, so even cover of 0.9 or less need not make a Zero a very risky proposition. In fact, Zeros with cover below 1 can offer the best deals for the individual investor, because institutions that invest in Zeros often impose a rule barring any investment where cover is less than 1. This means that demand for these shares is less and their prices may be anomalously low, and yields correspondingly high, compared with other fixed interest investments.

There are many different Zeros with different redemption dates, so it is possible to buy shares that will be redeemed in successive years. This means you can use the tax-free capital gains on Zeros (within your annual gains tax exemption) as tax-free income. Say you invested in five Zeros maturing five, six, seven, eight, and nine years from now. You would invest in each share the sum necessary to produce a capital gain of £3,000 in each of those years. So long as your taxable gains in each year did not exceed your £6,300 allowance, the 'income' would be tax-free. So you would have provided yourself with a £3,000 tax-free income for five years.

Tables are produced every day by marketmakers Natwest Securities and Warburgs giving all the relevant data on Zeros, and any stockbroker should be able to get copies of these for you.

Verdict: A series of Zeros can provide a tax-free income, or can meet a known fixed outlay such as school fee payments. Either way, they provide a high, reasonably secure tax-free return, and because the shares are quoted on the stock market, you can get access to your capital at any time if you need to do so.

As the example of Zeros shows, fixed interest can generate capital gains through the reinvestment of interest. The evidence of the past is that this is rarely a worthwhile strategy if you have to pay tax on the interest. But if you can avoid tax then the returns can be satisfactory, especially taking into account the relatively low risk.

In general, fixed interest investment is best used to generate spendable income or to accumulate capital over relatively short periods. If you plan to save regularly over a period of 10 years or more, though, all the evidence shows that plans with at least some equity investment have produced much higher returns in the past and there is no reason to suppose that they will not do so in the future as well. Such equity plans with a moderate level of risk are featured in the next chapter.

6 || *Tax-free Savings with Moderate Risk*

Savings schemes linked to deposits or fixed interest can secure your capital and provide reasonable returns depending on the level of interest rates. And if you accumulate or reinvest the interest, you can obtain growth in your capital.

But if you want higher returns on your savings you need to take on – at least to some extent – the higher risk associated with equity investment. With equities you get prospects of an increase in the capital value and of rising income from your capital as well. So in the long run savings schemes linked to shares almost always produce much higher returns than those linked to deposits or fixed interest, as shown in Table 7 (see page 39).

The future path of stock market prices is largely unpredictable, so such savings schemes are not suitable for the short term (periods of five years or less) unless you are prepared to accept that you might end up with less than you would have had in a safer scheme or, in the worst case scenario, actually suffer a loss on your capital or monthly savings.

But not all equity investments are high-risk and this chapter looks at schemes where the risk is moderate but the tax-free returns can be expected to outpace those from deposits or fixed interest over periods of over five years.

A Fixed Interest–Equity Split

One obvious way of boosting your return without taking on too much extra risk is to divide your money between fixed interest and equity investments. You can do this for yourself in normal investments. For example, you could divide your savings between an equity and a fixed interest unit trust. But if you want to avoid tax, you need to use a Personal Equity Plan or a friendly society savings plan (see below).

50–50 PEPs

Most PEPs are either pure equity (investing only in shares) or pure fixed interest (investing only in bonds), but a few managers offer PEPs where your money is divided between equity and fixed interest. The result is a plan which produces a relatively high income, up to twice as much as you would normally get from shares alone, but with prospects for some capital growth as well.

If we took the average returns from equity and fixed interest investment in the past and assumed you earned those returns on half your money, then the average annual return over the five years and 10 years to December 1994 from a 50–50 equity–fixed interest investment would have been 10.7% and 11.3% respectively. Deduct, say, 1.25% a year for management charges and you would have had annual returns of 9.45% and 10.05%.

That is the theory, but there are two major qualifications to add. The first is that the past decade has seen exceptionally high returns from both fixed interest and equity investments, and returns may well be lower in future. The second is that since funds of this type have not been in existence in the past we need to be cautious in projecting what may happen in the future. For instance, some managers specifically say they will vary the proportions of the capital invested in equity and fixed interest investment from time to time. This should give more scope for improving returns, assuming that the managers can switch money into shares when the stock market is doing well and return more capital to fixed interest when they can secure attractive high returns. But they may also make mistakes, thus generating lower returns than a simple 50–50 split. Moreover managers choose different types of share: some aim to invest only in shares in large, relatively secure companies – like utilities – with above-average dividend yields; others invest more widely in higher-yielding shares, which are normally more risky, and in smaller companies, which are doubly so. So the actual element of risk in the equity section of the fund will depend on the managers' choice of shares, and the overall level of risk will also depend on how much discretion the managers have to vary the proportions of the capital invested in equity and fixed interest.

These mixed equity–fixed interest plans do have considerable attractions if you think you may need access to your cash within five years. With pure equity schemes, a stock market crash just when you wanted to take money out could push you into loss, but with a 50–50 plan you are less likely to suffer a capital loss.

For many cautious savers, too, these plans offer a good longer-term savings medium. Pure equity plans usually produce the best payouts over terms of 15 to 25 years, but not everyone will be happy with the thrills and spills along the way. And depending on what you plan to use your savings for, it may be more important to you to avoid the spills than to get the highest possible returns.

One example of a savings objective where security can outweigh the desire for the highest returns is a savings plan designed to pay off the capital debt on a mortgage. You may aim to pay off the debt at the end of a specific period – say 20 years. But in practice, changes in your circumstances could well mean you want to pay off part or all of the debt earlier. If you think this is likely, then a pure equity plan, with its risk of sudden drops in value, is not the ideal scheme. However a 50–50 equity–fixed interest scheme is a better proposition if you have medium- to longer-term plans for a capital sum but may also need to withdraw your money earlier without too much risk of disaster.

These 50–50 plans could also be used to damp down the level of risk as the end of your savings term gets closer. You could start your 25-year savings plan in a pure equity PEP, and in year 20 transfer from this to a 50–50 plan. This would 'lock in' some of the gains achieved over the previous 20 years.

PEPs of this type may also be useful to generate income in retirement. You will get a higher income from corporate bond PEPs than from 50–50 plans, but it never makes sense to invest for more income than you need. So if you can get by with a somewhat lower income than a corporate bond PEP produces, the 50–50 plan will give more scope for capital growth and for a rising income in the future.

As with other PEPs, the annual limit on investment is £6,000 per person. Income and capital gains are tax-exempt whether these are accumulated or you withdraw cash from the plan.

As with other PEPs, the factors to assess in choosing a plan are charges and management skill. You should aim to pay no more than 3% in initial charges and 1.25% in annual charges. Many plans offer regular savings options from £100 per month as well as lump sum investments.

Verdict: 50–50 plans combining equity and fixed interest within the tax-exempt form of a PEP offer the prospect of good returns and moderate risk – an ideal combination for cautious investors. Even so, fluctuations in financial markets mean you should really have a minimum term of five years in mind.

Friendly plans, but high charges

Another type of tax-exempt plan that often offers a 50–50 Equity–Fixed Interest split is the monthly savings plan offered by a special category of tax-exempt friendly societies. Plans with contributions of up to £25 per month are specifically exempt from tax. Investments with such plans are not subject to income or capital gains tax and there is no personal tax liability on the payout.

But these plans are much less flexible than PEPs. They are 10-year savings plans, and there are usually both surrender penalties and a possible tax charge if the plans are encashed before their 10th anniversary. Also, because the maximum contributions are low, the costs and charges on these plans are relatively high. So if you were to compare a PEP with a friendly society plan, assuming the same annual growth rate, the PEP would come out well ahead, although you should remember that you cannot save as little as £25 per month in a PEP.

These plans may also be taken out by parents or grandparents for the benefit of a child. The child does not become entitled to the proceeds until either the plan matures at the end of 10 years or the child reaches the age of 18. If the plan matures before this, the accumulated capital can be left within the plan until the child's 18th birthday. This may appear an attractive way of building up a small next-egg for a child, but don't forget the high charges. Over many 10-year periods in the past, even taking into account these plans' tax exemption, you would have built up a larger nest-egg with a taxable unit trust regular savings plan than you would have obtained from a friendly society plan.

Verdict: the packaging of friendly society plans is attractive, but the value of tax exemption is eroded by high costs and charges. Friendly society plan promoters make a virtue of their plans' modest contribution level: as it is well within their means, people can be easily persuaded to sign up for a plan. However, if you can afford to save more than £25 per month then you should certainly consider other options which are likely to offer better value for money.

Stock Market Schemes

Option income funds: a high tax-free income
One specialist type of PEP provides a very high income which, like all other PEP income, is tax-exempt. These funds – sometimes referred to as 'option income funds' – hold half their money in the shares of large companies, but use derivatives to generate a high additional income from the rest of the fund's cash. Essentially, the funds obtain income from the dividends on the shares they own, from cash deposits and from the derivatives transactions.

The way these work is complex, but the managers aim to sell the 'volatility premium' that attaches to shares. Most derivatives are designed to capture an upwards or downwards movement in shares or other assets. The pricing of these contracts, as compared with the prices of the shares themselves, reveals the risk premium investors currently consider realistic for shares in general. By engaging in balancing derivative transactions that create exposure to profits if the market rises and equal exposure to losses if it falls – so that the fund has taken on no additional risk overall – the fund can capture the volatility premium itself in the form of extra income.

With dividend yields at about 4%, short-term interest rates between 5% and 10%, and equity volatility premiums between 12% and 15%, a fund of this type should theoretically be capable of generating an annualized income of some 10–12% a year before management charges.

Option income funds are a relatively new concept in investment in the UK so it is not yet established whether such returns can be achieved over a period of years without incurring risks to capital. In theory, so long as the fund holds 50% of its capital in a portfolio of shares, then it should show some capital growth over the longer term. But if the managers make mistakes with their derivative strategies these gains could be eroded. And these funds will certainly not produce capital gains at anything like the level of funds which invest 100% in shares.

That said, these funds produce about the highest tax-exempt income going and if you really need to generate a high income on some of your capital they are worth considering.

As with other PEPs, you may invest up to £6,000 in any one tax year, though you may also (as with other PEPs) transfer money from existing PEPs to these high-income funds if you wish to boost your income.

Verdict: Option income funds generate a very high income and, if the managers deliver what they promise, should also generate some capital growth over a period of five years or more. So they are a useful way of boosting the income from your capital.

International equity funds: a widespread investment in quality shares

Over the years, the investment records of different types of fund have shown large variations both in the average returns they produce and in the average price variations or volatility. Equity funds that invest internationally in large companies have been shown to have records of steadier growth, with less variability in price, than 'specialist' funds which focus on just one type of share or shares in just one country. This is obvious enough if you think about it: developed countries are very unlikely to be affected by exactly the same economic influences at the same time. So, for example, when the American economy is doing well, Japan's may be in poor shape, while the main European economies may be somewhere in between. So if shares in these countries respond to these economic developments, a fund investing equally in shares in each of these countries will experience lower overall variations in the total value of its investments than any one of three funds investing in Japan, America or Europe.

It is important, though, that the managers stick to large established companies, since the evidence also shows that shares in smaller companies are more volatile in price no matter which of the world's equity markets you consider.

Another factor that is 'averaged' by an international fund is changes in currency exchange rates, which has a similar effect of damping down fluctuations in the value of its investments.

International equity funds can be divided into three distinct types. First, there is the very diversified fund where the managers aim to replicate closely the weightings held by individual countries within the world index. The world index is constructed by adding the value of all shares quoted in each market: so, for example, at the end of 1994 the UK accounted for under 10% of the total capitalization of shares in the world index. A genuinely international diversified fund would therefore hold less than 10% of its investments in UK shares. Only a few UK funds adopt this strategy.

The second type is one where the managers ignore these weightings and simply pick the markets and shares they consider most promising, which may involve having a large percentage of assets in one country or region at any one time.

Far more UK funds adopt a third strategy of having around 50% of their assets in UK shares and then dividing the rest between other countries roughly in accordance with their weightings in the world index. This is in fact the only approach they can adopt if they want to run a fund in which you can invest tax-free within the PEP rules. These require that a minimum of 50% is kept in UK/EU shares at all times.

So an international fund, within a PEP, usually holds at least 20% or 30% of its assets in UK shares, a further 20% or 30% in European shares and the balance in American, Japanese and other shares. Usually – but not always, and this is something the sales brochure will reveal – most of the money is invested in larger companies.

As Table 15 shows, funds of this type have been a rewarding investment over many periods in the past. Many investment managers and advisers would argue that a fund of this type is in fact the ideal first step in equity investment, because of its wide spread and balance of risk. The only drawback to these funds is that they usually produce relatively low dividend income, as compared with funds that invest only in UK shares because the UK is something of an exception in world stock markets: UK companies tend to pay larger dividends, and dividend income forms a larger part of the expected return from shares. In Japan, for example, investors expect returns in the form of capital gains so income from dividends is not generally regarded as so important. This means that almost all funds investing outside the UK will produce a lower dividend income than UK-only funds. This is a drawback in that you are gaining less benefit from the PEP tax exemptions if a larger part of your total return comes in the form of capital gain, since you can in any case make up to £6,300 of capital gains each year without paying any tax on your taxable investments. Many UK advisers now tend to advocate PEP investments that generate income for this reason.

Table 15: Returns from international equity unit trusts

Results of a £1,000 investment over periods to 1st December 1995. Offer to offer prices for average fund with gross income reinvested.

Period (years)	Value	Annual return
5	£1,937	14.1%
10	£3,618	13.7%
15	£13,580	19.0%

Source: Micropal

Verdict: PEP funds investing internationally must keep at least 50% in UK/EU securities, but their wide spread of investments means they do have a lower risk than one-country stock market funds. As with other funds, you need to pay attention to charges since these vary from 1% to as much as 2.5% a year.

Equity income trusts: higher income, and gains too
One category of UK unit trusts has, over many years, consistently provided higher returns to investors than other types of unit trust investing only in UK shares. These 'equity income' trusts invest only in shares and aim to provide a level of dividend income higher than the average for all shares, and in addition to produce rising income and capital growth in the future.

This may seem an ambitious set of objectives, but the statistics clearly show that this type of trust has beaten its UK rivals handsomely over most periods in the past, as shown by Table 16.

Trusts of this type qualify as investments within a PEP, and many funds which have achieved excellent returns over periods in the past can be bought as lump sum investments within a PEP or used with a regular savings plan.

So far, nobody has come up with a complete explanation of why this one type of trust does better than its rivals, but the most widely accepted theory is that the income objectives of these trusts force the managers to adopt a successful investment strategy. The point is that shares which offer a higher than average level of dividend yield can do so for one of two main reasons: either the company is heading for trouble, in which case it will not be able to sustain the current level of dividends in future, or investors in general have become overly pessimistic about the prospects for the company and its future dividend payments, and this has resulted in an unjustified fall in the share price. If managers of equity income trusts buy shares in the second type of company, then sooner or later other investors will come to realize that the prospects are better than they thought, more investors will buy the shares and their price will rise. An inevitable consequence of the rise in price is that the dividend yield on the shares will fall. Since the managers of equity income trusts have constantly to watch the dividend yield on the whole portfolio they manage, they are under pressure to sell shares after they have achieved a good profit, and to look for other shares where they can repeat the exercise.

Whatever the reason, these trusts have achieved both a higher than average level of income and a higher level of capital growth

Table 16: Returns from equity income unit trusts

Offer-to-offer prices for average fund in each sector. Gross income reinvested. Periods to 1st December 1995.

Results of saving £100 per month

Average fund in sector	Period in years			
	5	10	15	20
UK equity income	£8,503	£22,779	£73,046	£194,332
UK equity growth	£8,537	£21,134	£59,567	£148,360

Results of investment of £1,000

UK equity income	£1,997	£3,957	£13,174	£30,418
UK equity growth	£2,023	£3,282	£9,181	£21,105

Source: Micropal

than other UK-investing trusts, so they are clearly worth considering both for lump sum investments and regular savings plans.

If you want an immediate tax-exempt income, then you can draw it from the dividends, but if you do not need income you can simply reinvest all the dividends to boost your capital.

Verdict: Equity income unit trusts are somewhat more volatile than international trusts. But their history of high returns means they are very attractive, especially when – as in a PEP – no tax is paid on dividends.

Bricks and Mortar

Unless you run your own pension fund, an investment in property cannot be tax-exempt, but UK taxpayers do have valuable concessions on property ownership.

Owning and renting property

You pay no capital gains tax if you make a profit on your home – however much this is – so long as the property is your 'principal private residence'. In the 1960s, 1970s and much of the 1980s, when property prices rose steeply, people were able to make huge tax-free gains. All you had to do was buy the biggest house you could afford on a large mortgage, and whenever possible sell and trade up to an even bigger house on a larger mortgage. Up until 1988 this strategy produced almost effortless tax-free capital gains for millions of homeowners.

In 1988 the party came to an end. A normal cyclical downturn in house price – a common occurrence during the previous 20 years – was turned into a much deeper and more prolonged fall by a change in Government policies, firstly in allowing mortgage interest rates to rise to unprecedented levels, and secondly in reducing tax relief on mortgage interest from 25% to 20% and then 15% on the first £30,000 of a mortgage. Though house prices in the North of England and Scotland have recovered well since 1990, prices in the southern half of the country have remained depressed. Even in 1995 nearly a million homeowners were still caught in the 'negative equity trap', where the amount outstanding on their mortgage was larger than the value of their home at current market prices. A generation's faith in property as a worthwhile investment has been shattered.

Most economists forecast a dull residential property market for many years to come, partly for demographic reasons: there are not enough new entrants at the bottom of the housing market ladder to push up prices higher up; and the increase in property available for private renting has reduced potential demand further.

So property as a source of capital gain does not seem as attractive as it once was. Of course, for many people, it will still be cheaper to own than to rent. In making a calculation of the relative costs, though, you should never overlook the indirect costs of property, including the cost of maintenance and insurance. On average these are likely to amount to at least 2% a year over a 20-year period.

The tax system also gives benefits to ownership of second properties, provided these are let out. The concessions also apply to second homes in the form of furnished holiday accommodation for short-term letting. Provided you let out such a property for at least 70 days a year, and make it available for rent for at least 140 days, then for tax purposes the purchase of the asset is treated as a trade rather than an investment. This has considerable tax advantages. First, all the expenses you incur in relation to the property will be deductible from the rental income. These expenses include the interest on any loan raised to purchase the property. In effect this means you can get unlimited tax relief on mortgage interest on purchase of a second property, so long as it generates sufficient rental income to pay the interest. Second, if the expenses (excluding loan interest) are greater than the income and you have a loss, this loss can be offset against your other taxable income and thereby reduce the tax you pay on it. Third, pre-trading expenses can likewise be deducted from other income. Fourth, the purchase can be used to 'roll over' capital gains, which means you can defer – until the property itself is sold – the payment of tax on previous capital gains. Fifth, the income from the property is treated as earned income and you may make personal pension contributions and offset them against this income, thus reducing the tax payable on it, even if you are employed and are a member of a company pension scheme.

Until 1995 furnished holiday property benefited from larger reliefs than purchase of other property for letting, but from April 1995 the rules have been brought largely into line. The same concessions now apply to all properties for let, including those abroad, although the offsets against other income allowed for furnished holiday lets are slightly higher than for other types of property. A new concession is that if you cannot use up a loss from the property business in one year, it may be carried forward to be set against letting profits in future years.

These tax concessions can make investment in this type of property an attractive proposition. But don't overlook the significant risks. You may not always be able to get a rental income: it may be hard to find a suitable tenant or tenants, or a severe recession may mean that people simply cannot afford the rent you need – which could be serious if you need that income in order to pay the interest on a loan you took out to buy the property. Also, when it comes to selling, property is by nature an illiquid asset: it may take months or even years to sell if you want to achieve your chosen price target. Finally, the transaction expenses on purchase and sale are high. With estate agency fees, fees on loan agreements and so forth, purchase and sale fees can easily amount to between 3% and 4% of the purchase price of a property.

Some individuals certainly do 'make a go' of running properties of this kind for profit, but they recognize that it is a business and needs the dedication and discipline of any other business venture if it is to prove successful. It is not something to be approached in a part-time fashion.

Verdict: Owning your own home is something most people will want to do sooner or later, but as much for practical as investment reasons. The investment reasons for ownership are certainly not as strong as they were, though over a long period of time owning your own home is likely to produce some tax-free capital gains. Investment in additional properties should be regarded as a business venture.

7 | *Going All Out for Growth*

Investment managers who are seeking to damp down the risk inherent in equity investment use terms like 'prudent', 'cautious' and 'balanced' in relation to their investment strategies. But the evidence of the past also shows quite clearly that higher risk is rewarded by higher return as well as by greater day-to-day price fluctuations.

The Pros and Cons of Higher Risks

Can you afford to take on these higher risks? Your own character may be one factor to take into account: how soundly do you sleep when the value of your savings bobs up and down? The significance of psychological attitudes to investment risk has been summed up in the saying: 'If you don't know who you are, the stock market is an expensive place to find out.' But there are some objective components too, the two main ones being:

- The more you've got, the more you can afford to lose. If you have only a small amount, whether it is capital or monthly savings, then avoiding the risk of loss is likely to be a high priority. If you have a large capital sum or monthly savings, you can place some of it in riskier investments without incurring too much personal risk: you are likely to be able to ride out any temporary dip in the market because you have other capital you can draw on, and even if your chosen high-risk investment does turn out to be a disaster, it has only affected a part and not all of your assets.
- The longer the intended timescale of your saving or invest-

ment the more risk you can afford to take. Refer back to Table 6 on page 35. After 15 to 20 years a crash in the price of a high-risk investment, cutting its value by 20% or even 30% overnight, could still leave you with a larger capital sum than you would have had from a lower-risk, lower-growth investment that had not suffered such a crash.

A less objective but equally important factor is that higher-risk investing is more fun. The idea that saving or investing can be enjoyable may worry you. If so, your character is probably not well suited to high-risk investing. That said, there do seem to be differences between the ways in which men and women approach the issue of risk. Most men enjoy the intellectual challenge of trying to choose the right share, stock market or fund, but also clearly enjoy the uncertain aspect of investment that brings in the gambling element. Women, on the other hand, often take quite substantial risks without acknowledging that this is what they are doing, as if in itself their faith in a particular share or investment was sufficient justification for investing a large sum. There is no right or wrong in this, but it is important to be aware of what you are doing.

Higher Risk Investments

Higher risk in the Stock Market

Stock markets, both in the UK and in other countries, provide many different types of investment, some of which offer considerably greater risk than that involved in investing in established, blue chip companies. In this section we will consider four higher-risk stock market investments that can be held within a tax-exempt PEP. The extent of the extra risk is not always easy to quantify, but it is clearly greater than for the stock market investments discussed in the previous chapter.

Smaller company funds: While large, long-established companies rarely fail, small companies can and often do go bust. Research shows that in most stock markets investment in smaller companies is both more rewarding and more risky than investment in larger companies. This is intuitively obvious. A large company cannot easily double its sales from, say, £1,000 million to £2,000 million, but a small one can relatively easily double its sales from £10 million to £20 million; likewise with profits and dividends. The reasons why small companies are more vulnerable are many and various, but the most important seem to be business risk and financial factors. Small companies are much more often dependent on one product than large companies, which means they are more exposed to competitors, changes in markets and so forth. Moreover, most small companies sell a high proportion of their goods in domestic markets whereas large companies usually sell more abroad. Small companies are therefore more vulnerable to recessions at home. As for finance, small companies often have higher debts in relation to their capital – these loans are needed to finance their rapid rates of growth. This can lead to financial crises when the rate of growth slows down or is interrupted by recessions, supply problems or other factors.

Professional investment managers offer many specialist funds investing in smaller companies in the UK, America, Japan, Europe and on a worldwide basis. Not all of these funds qualify for investment of the full amount in a PEP. Investments in unit or investment trusts that invest exclusively in non-UK/EU shares may only account for £1,500 of the annual £6,000 PEP allowance. But funds investing more than 50% of their assets in UK or EU smaller companies do qualify for the full £6,000 allowance.

Over the long-term – 10 years or more – funds investing in smaller companies tend to outpace funds investing in larger ones. The longer the investment period, the more marked the superior results from smaller companies have been in the past, and there seems little reason to doubt that this tendency will persist into the future. So there is certainly a case for placing part of your savings or investments in funds of this type.

Specialist sector funds: A second category of higher-risk funds is 'specialist sector funds'. These restrict their investment to one type of business, for example healthcare or technology, usually on a worldwide basis, which means they will normally only qualify for a £1,500 investment within a £6,000 PEP. Some funds have been launched investing only in recent European privatizations, and these qualify for a full £6,000 PEP investment.

The evidence from specialist sector funds has been much more mixed than that from smaller company funds. Some sector funds have done well for short periods, while some have done very badly. There is little evidence of sustained and consistent superior results from these funds, so it is much more a matter of picking the right time to invest, and of taking your profits and moving on to something else.

Overseas-investing funds: A third category of higher-risk investments is overseas-investing funds. In any year you may only invest £1,500 out of a £6,000 PEP allowance in funds investing outside the UK/EU, unless the fund manager has chosen to adopt a policy whereby at least 50% of the fund's assets will be held in UK/EU shares at all times. So you can put at least some of your tax-exempt PEP money into overseas-investing funds.

The world's stock markets rarely move in step, so usually there is a market somewhere in the world that is rising fast, just as there is usually one that is falling fast. There are two valid approaches to overseas markets and funds. You can decide that you will put money in and leave it invested for a long period because the prospects for growth in the country or market justify long-term confidence in obtaining high returns. Or you can take short-term decisions and buy and sell units in these funds with the aim of making quick profits. Both approaches are possible within a PEP. But if you want to buy and sell on a short-term basis you need to select a plan manager offering a sufficiently wide range of international funds to give you enough scope.

Self-select PEPs/Single Company PEPs: The fourth way of adopting a higher-risk investment strategy with stock market investments within a PEP is to choose them yourself. There are two ways in which you can do this. You can set up a self-select PEP with most stockbroking firms and make your own investment decisions. Several firms offer low-cost plans where there is only a nominal set-up fee and no annual management charge. But you will incur stockbrokers' dealing charges on every transaction and, at around 1.65%, stockbrokers' commission rates on individual share deals within most self-select PEPs are about eight times higher than the commissions paid by unit and investment trusts on their much larger deals. This is certainly a handicap for the individual investor choosing his or her own shares, as compared with the professional investment manager, but against this you can set a saving of between 1% and 1.5% in annual management fees which are normal with professionally managed funds such as unit and investment trusts and are not charged in the better-value self-select PEPs.

The second way is to put money into single company PEPs. In addition to the £6,000 a year you are allowed to invest in a 'general' PEP, you are also allowed to invest up to £3,000 in a single company PEP in each tax year. As the name suggests, all the money must go into the shares of just one company. You can operate single company PEPs through a stockbroker – in which case you choose your own shares, and can sell one and buy another at any time. Alternatively you can use the single company PEP facilities set up by many major companies whose shares are quoted on the Stock Exchange. This is a cheaper option, since charges on company-sponsored PEPs are nominal and there is virtually no cost of buying. But if you want to sell your shares and then buy other shares within a PEP you will first have to transfer your PEP into a self-select plan.

Provided you are prepared to devote the time and effort to managing your own stock market investments, there is no reason why you should not achieve good results. But if things go wrong, you will have nobody to blame but yourself.

Self-select PEPs were designed for investors who already hold large quantities of shares, so that each year they could transfer £6,000 worth into a PEP and pay no taxes on dividends or future capital gains. Single company PEPs are a useful way for investors who already hold a share portfolio to gradually convert it into a tax-free form over a period of years.

Academic studies have shown that you need to own between 15 and 20 individual shares in order to reduce the average level of risk on these shares to the average of the stock market as a whole, as represented by a representative share index. If you own fewer shares, it means you will be incurring a higher level of risk, and though this may correspond with higher returns, this may not be true of the shares you have chosen. If you do build up a share portfolio, be prepared to commit time and energy to looking after it. For most people it makes more sense to use PEPs linked to collective investment funds. Provided you pick funds with low charges, the costs involved in buying and selling units in these funds need be no higher than the costs of buying and selling shares.

Verdict: The evidence of the past suggests that it is well worth taking on the higher risks inherent in more growth-oriented equity funds in view of the higher returns they tend to achieve. But be wary of plans that levy high annual charges.

Geared investments

The investments discussed in the previous section involve a slightly higher degree of risk than the average as represented by a stock market index. This section covers investments that generate additional returns, and higher risk, through gearing.

In its simplest form gearing can be achieved by borrowing money. Say you had £10,000 to invest and borrowed an extra £5,000 from a bank and invested that too. Then – ignoring for the moment the interest on the loan – if the value of the shares went up by 10% from £15,000 to £16,500, your gain would not be 10% but 15% because the amount you owed would still be £5,000, so that after allowing for the repayment of the loan your profit would be £1,500 on £10,000. So long as the rate of interest you pay on the loan is lower than the rate of return you earn on the investment, borrowing money will enable you to generate extra capital from your investments. But it also involves extra risk. If there is a market crash and the value of the £15,000 of shares falls to £10,000, you still owe £5,000 to the bank and have suffered a 50% loss of your capital.

This is an extreme example. In practice, most people use gearing through their mortgage arrangements. If you have an interest-only mortgage together with a savings plan designed to repay the mortgage at the end of a savings period, then you are using gearing. By leaving the debt outstanding rather than paying it off bit by bit from those savings, you hope to obtain a rate of return on the savings greater than the interest rate you pay on the mortgage. In practice, over long periods like 20 years, savings linked to the stock market have always earned a higher return than a mortgage interest rate, so this type of gearing has consistently paid off in the past. Most people can accept gearing in this form, because it is related to small regular savings, but would consider it highly speculative to borrow money in order to invest. But if you analyse the reasons why many investment trusts have produced better results than similar unit trusts over long periods, a major factor is that most investment trusts are geared – they borrow money to add to the shareholders' money they invest in the stock market.

In America the notion of borrowing money for investment is commonplace, and in recent years UK stockbrokers have started to offer credit facilities to their customers. The rate of interest charged by a stockbroker is likely to be slightly higher than you would pay to a bank if you were a longstanding customer with a good credit rating.

Split-capital investment trusts: There are some collective stock market investments that create gearing in a more sophisticated, structured way. These split-capital investment trusts, like other investment trusts, raise money from shareholders and invest it on the stock market. But unlike other investment trusts, they have more than one type of share, and there is also a fixed date when the trust will be wound up, its investments sold and the cash distributed to shareholders.

Some trusts have capital shares which get all the capital from the trust's investments, and income shares which are entitled to all the income from the trust's investments but get no capital repayment at all at redemption. The owners of the capital shares get a geared capital return. The net asset value of a capital share – the value of the assets divided by the number of capital shares – will rise and fall by a larger percentage than the value of the trust's total assets. Capital shareholders are earning growth on a larger sum of money than they invested. Likewise, the income shareholders get a geared income investment. Even though they will get nothing when the trust is wound up, in the meantime they get all the income, and because the trust invests mainly in shares this income will also rise over the years. So they will get a very high income indeed over a period of time. This type of income share is termed an 'annuity income share', because one way of looking at it is to say that all the capital you invest in such an income share is converted into income over its remaining life to redemption.

Split capital investment trusts can include other types of share too. Some income shares, often called traditional income shares, do get a capital repayment at redemption, often the price at which they were first issued, and these shares also get all the income from the trust's investments. Often the market price of these shares is above their redemption value, so there will be a capital loss if you hold them to redemption, but in the meantime you get a very high income. With another type of share, the ordinary income share, you get not only all the income but the rights to all the capital too once a different class of shares, the Zero Dividend Preference shares, are paid off at maturity. These ordinary income shares – sometimes referred to as geared ordinary income shares – in fact have both income gearing and capital gearing.

All these split-capital shares, with the exception of Zeros, may be included within PEPs. To buy such shares within a PEP, you will usually have to set up a self-select PEP and get a stockbroker to buy the shares you want. But sometimes managers who are launching a new trust of this type set up a PEP facility at no cost.

Because most people need not pay capital gains tax if they time the sale of their investments carefully, it will rarely make sense to hold capital shares within a PEP. But if you need a high income, it may make sense to hold one or other of the types of income share in a PEP. In fact the higher the income the share produces, the more advantageous it is to hold it within a PEP, because the immediate income tax saving will be that much greater.

Verdict: Highly geared investments like split investment trust capital shares can generate very high returns at over 15% a year. But the risk is also high and it is important to try to avoid investing when the stock market level is high. Placing split-capital trust income shares inside a PEP maximizes the income tax savings and can be useful for retired people who need a high income from their money.

Higher risk in new ventures

Investing in small companies is risky enough, but riskier still is investing in brand-new small companies. A high proportion of all new businesses fail and in many cases shareholders lose all their money, because other creditors' and banks' claims usually absorb all that is left.

Still, new small companies are the ones that generate the majority of all new employment opportunities, so the Government of any country with a high unemployment rate is bound to see some merit in helping new companies to get off the ground. Small business lobbyists in the UK have also claimed that there is a 'financing gap' because the large investment institutions will not invest small sums in brand-new companies.

There are currently two tax-favoured schemes aimed at small new companies, both recently introduced: the Enterprise Investment Scheme (EIS) and the Venture Capital Trust (VCT). Both the EIS and the VCT currently suffer from a problem that is normal for relatively new schemes. The Inland Revenue is always so concerned about possible loss of tax revenue through these schemes that it makes the rules governing them excessively complex – in some cases rendering a scheme almost unworkable, or at least imposing high costs on schemes that do meet the Inland Revenue requirements. Both the PEP and the Business Expansion Scheme required two Budgets' worth of amendments to the initial regulations before they became usable. It may therefore be some time before the EIS or VCT can be used effectively by the average investor.

The EIS is focused on brand-new small companies. If you invest in EIS shares you get tax relief at 20% on up to £100,000 of investment in any one tax year. This means that if you invest £10,000, you will get a reduction in your income tax bill (or a tax repayment) of £2,000. The money must remain invested for five years, and after this you pay no capital gains tax on any profit on a sale of shares. If the company does go bust, then you may write off a further 20% against your tax bill – in other words, claim a further £1,600 tax reduction from the initial net cost of £8,000 (after the initial tax relief). But if you sell your shares within five years you will be liable to capital gains tax on any profit and will also have the initial income tax relief clawed back by the Inland Revenue.

You may also defer a capital gain on the sale of an investment or asset by investing a sum equal to the taxable gain through the EIS. The gain is then deferred until the EIS investment is sold, and is extinguished if the company fails.

The effect of these tax concessions is that, if the business goes bust, you lose 60% or 80% of your investment, but if it is a success you pay no tax on your profits.

There are many detailed rules and restructions on the EIS, the most important of which are:

- You are not entitled to tax relief if you own or control more than 30% of the shares in the company.
- The company may not raise more than £1 million in share capital through an EIS issue.
- You must subscribe for new shares in order to get tax relief on the investment.
- Shares are exempt from capital gains tax only on their first disposal.
- Companies do not qualify for EIS relief if they engage in a number of defined trades, such as land and property dealing, banking and insurance, oil extraction or leasing.
- EIS tax relief will be lost and 'clawed back' by the Inland Revenue if the company ceases to be a qualifying company within five years of making the investment.
- There is a further set of anti-avoidance rules designed to prevent you and members of your family setting up a company and using it as a collective tax shelter.

The EIS was launched in 1994, so as yet there is no useful data on the success or failure of EIS investments. However, a similar scheme called the Business Expansion Scheme, which ran for several years up to 1993, produced a large crop of failures. It is worth noting that many of these failures were companies promoted as relatively low-risk investments because they owned and rented residential property. The crash in residential property prices between 1989 and 1993 meant that even at the end of the five-year term of the BES investment, many of these companies were likely to produce losses for their investors.

Investment promoters have attempted, as they did with the BES, to design investment schemes that obtain the tax advantages of the EIS but minimize the risk. So there are two types of EIS investment: genuine high-risk, ground-floor investment in new enterprises, and tax-shelter schemes designed by investment promoters. The latter may provide reasonable net returns without excessive risk, but a large part of the tax relief offered by such schemes is often absorbed in the promoter's charges, professional fees and other costs. So you need to examine any such scheme very carefully indeed, paying particular attention to all the small print and the costs and charges.

As for genuine EIS investments, you may come across opportunities to invest in new ventures being organized with the help of local accountants, lawyers or stockbrokers. Perhaps the best way to invest in such ventures is as one of a small group of investors, each of whom has some specific expertise or contacts as well as cash to contribute to the business.

However you find them, EIS investments will be high-risk and there will always be a possibility that you will lose every penny you invest. With this type of investment, you really must invest only money you can afford to lose.

Verdict: Ground-floor investment in new companies produces the highest returns in the equity sector. If you back a successful company from its inception your gain can be measured in thousands rather than hundreds of percent. But the risk of total loss is high, so you need to devote great care to selecting investments. It also makes sense to spread the risk by investing in several companies.

New tax shelter for venture capital

Venture Capital Trusts are also a recent development: the first trusts appeared only in 1995. In order to qualify for tax relief, these trusts must hold 70% of their assets in unquoted securities and at least 30% must be in unquoted shares. For the purposes of this definition, shares listed on the Alternative Investment Market are regarded as unquoted. A trust may not invest more than £1m in the securities of any one company, and no individual company in which a VCT invests may have assets of over £10m before the issue of new shares to VCTs. VCTs themselves must have their own shares listed on the Stock Exchange.

Provided a trust meets these requirements, investors in new

shares issued by a VCT – the limit is £100,000 worth in any one tax year – may claim tax relief of 20% of the sum invested, reducing the cost of a £10,000 investment to £8,000. They may also claim deferral of the capital gains tax payable on any gain they have already made on other assets by investing a sum equal to the taxable gain in a VCT. Both concessions require the shares to be held for at least five years and the tax relief will be clawed back if the shares are disposed of earlier or if the VCT itself ceases to qualify. Provided the shares are held for five years, no income tax will be payable on any dividends received from the VCT, and no gains tax will be payable on the gain on the VCT shares sold.

If you have made a capital gain large enough for it to be taxable at 40%, then the combination of the gains tax deferral and the income tax relief means you get an initial rate of tax relief of 60% on a VCT investment. Of this, 40% is only deferred until the VCT shares themselves are sold.

A major drawback of VCTs is that your investment must be in the form of new shares issued by the VCT. There are many venture capital investment trusts already listed on the Stock Exchange which do not qualify for the VCT tax concessions, and their shares usually trade at a discount to the value of the trust's assets. In recent years the discount has been as high as 30% and as low as 15%. The discount tends to rise during recessions, since investors expect that some of a trust's investments will fail and that many of them will decline in value. In times of strong economic growth and stock market booms, the discount gets smaller because investors expect small companies to do well – and shares in some of the companies in which the trust has invested to be launched on the stock market at a much higher price than they are valued at as unquoted investments.

In general, then, you can expect to buy shares in a non-qualifying venture capital trust at a discount of between 15 and 20% to the value of their assets, and this discount is roughly equal to the initial tax relief on subscribing for new shares in a VCT with no discount. This reduces the relative attractions of the VCT, especially bearing in mind the minimum five-year holding period.

As for the deferral of capital gains tax on an existing gain, this concession applies not just to VCTs but also to any individual share that is listed on the Alternative Investment Market – the new market for shares of small new enterprises launched in 1995.

Verdict: The package of tax concessions for VCTs is not as good as it looks at first sight. If you have enough capital to do so, you get as good a set of tax breaks by investing through the EIS or on the Alternative Investment Market. And if you want a collective investment, then you should certainly consider existing venture capital investment trusts as well as VCTs.

High-risk property

Back in the 1980s one of those political wheezes to win credit for helping industry produced 'enterprise zones' – areas in which businesses benefit from lower rates on property. To encourage development of suitable property within these zones, investors were allowed to claim income tax relief on investment in new property within enterprise zones so long as the property was let to a suitable tenant. As is often the way with schemes launched with an overtly political purpose, things went wrong in some of the zones, and most of the benefit of the tax relief given to investors went into inflating the price of property within the zones, so many of the early investors found they had capital losses rather than profits on their investments.

The reason these properties attracted substantial sums was that there was no limit to the amount you could invest and still claim tax relief. So if you had a taxable income of £10m and had used up your entitlements to other tax shelters, investing in property in an enterprise zone was the obvious next step. Unlike most other tax shelters, too, enterprise zone property is an investment open to companies as well as individuals, and many private companies preferred to invest in property than pay corporation tax.

Few investors can afford a whole building in an enterprise zone, let alone in Canary Wharf where individual buildings can cost over £100m. So promoters formed Property Enterprise Trusts (PETs), which benefit from the same tax reliefs but allow groups of investors to share an investment in a building.

A major drawback with this type of investment is that if you sell it within 25 years there will be a clawback of some of the initial tax relief.

Verdict: These highly specialized investments should be approached with extreme caution.

Tax exemption grows on trees

For many years forestry benefited from a set of complex tax concessions. These were largely swept away and in exchange forestry was made tax-exempt.

Ownership of the land on which the trees grow is not tax-exempt; you may become liable to capital gains tax if you sell such land at a profit. But the income from selling timber is exempt from income tax, and sale of standing timber is exempt from capital gains tax. The land on which forests stand may count as a business asset for inheritance tax purposes, and thus qualify for 100% relief from the tax. The value of standing timber is, however, included in the taxable value of an estate.

Since you need to invest quite a substantial sum – usually over £100,000 – to obtain an interest in plantations of commercial size, this form of investment is of limited interest. In recent years, though, schemes have been set up to generate a tax-exempt income from woodlands. Promoters have set up trusts owning sizeable woodlands, in which individuals can invest relatively modest sums (£5,000 or so). The trusts buy mature conifer plantations and generate an income by felling trees and selling timber each year. The areas felled are replanted and, depending on assumptions concerning the rate of growth of the trees and on the future price of timber, the replanting is intended to ensure the plantations are at least as valuable at the end of the trust's life (usually between seven and 10 years) as when they were bought.

Whether it is actually possible to generate a tax-exempt income of as much as 7% in this way will probably only become clear when the first such trusts reach the end of their lives soon after the year 2000. But within the next few years data should become available on the progress of existing trusts, and if you are interested in such an investment it would be advisable to see how these trusts have performed so far.

Another important point is that forestry trusts are unregulated collective investments, which means they are not covered by any of the investor protection or regulation that applies to most of the investments described in this book.

Verdict: Forestry trusts need more time to demonstrate whether they can achieve their objectives without erosion of investors' capital.

A thing of beauty is tax-free for ever

Some tangible investments are taxable. Indeed, if the Inland Revenue considers that you are trading in them any tangibles may be taxable, in which case the profits on selling the items would be regarded as income subject to income tax. This is unlikely to happen to the average collector of stamps, coins or antiques, however.

The value of the things you collect during your life will be included in the valuation of your estate at death, so such items are potentially subject to inheritance tax. However, you need not pay capital gains tax if you sell items at a profit. Tangibles are classed by the Inland Revenue as 'chattels', on which there is no capital gains tax unless an item is sold for more than £6,300. In theory, if you break up a set to stay within this £6,300 limit – say you have an antique table and chairs and sell them separately so that no item exceeds £6,300 but you get £20,000 for the lot – then the Inland Revenue can assess the proceeds to capital gains tax: in theory, but, one suspects, not often in practice.

It is certainly possible to build up a collection of considerable value over a period of many years, whether in china, art, antiques, jewellery or other items. Few people who do this will be interested in selling their treasures, however, so the potential freedom from capital gains tax is unlikely to be of great interest to them.

As for the notion of collecting tangible items purely for profit, this idea has been promoted with almost universally disastrous results at intervals of about five years for the past 25 years. Georgian silver took over 20 years to reattain the prices at which it sold in the 1960s after a heavy burst of promotion of its value as an investment. Diamonds promoted as investments are worth less today than they were in the 1970s. Classic cars are worth less now than they were when they were being heavily promoted in the 1980s. Many other items have been the subject of fashions and promotions. The world of tangibles is prone to 'bubbles' – the original eighteenth-century term for an artificially inflated market, usually based on the actions of a small number of self-interested promoters.

Verdict: You will often meet people who have made sizeable gains on the stock market. You are unlikely to meet anyone who has made money by speculating in stamps, coins, wine, art and so forth. Unless you are a genuine collector, steer clear of tangibles.

8 ‖ *Specialist Tax Avoidance Schemes*

Very rich people may pay a lot of tax, but the tax they pay often represents a smaller proportion of their income than the top income tax rate of 40% would suggest. Certainly both capital gains tax and inheritance tax are now regarded by many professional advisers as voluntary taxes because there are so many legitimate ways of avoiding them.

Trusts

Trusts have played a major role in avoiding inheritance tax and its predecessors. Following bouts of anti-avoidance legislation, the taxation of trusts is now one of those jungles through which you really do need a qualified guide. Here we will focus on a couple of simple but effective uses of trusts as perfectly legitimate inheritance tax avoidance devices.

Most inheritance tax is collected not from the estates of very rich people but from the modestly well-off. Very wealthy people usually own a lot of business assets (which get 100% relief from tax) and can also afford to make lifetime gifts, which also escape tax provided that you live for seven years after making the gift. Modestly wealthy people need their capital to generate the income they live on, so they cannot afford to make lifetime gifts, and all their assets – including their home – count as part of their taxable estates. Given that the threshold for inheritance tax is £200,000, many married couples have estates in excess of this. Usually, realizing that whichever of them survives may need all the capital to pay for a nursing home in later years, they make wills leaving all their assets to each other. When the second partner dies, there is usually an estate well in excess of the threshold and therefore a sizeable inheritance tax bill.

The will trust

There is a simple trust solution to this: the will trust, which, as its name suggests, is a trust constituted through a will. The tax saving can be over £60,000 just using the simplest variant of this approach.

Arthur and Enid are in their late 70s. In addition to their house, worth £100,000, they have total assets which will be subject to inheritance tax of £300,000. They divide these assets so that each of them owns exactly half, and create a discretionary trust in each will whereby when the first spouse dies, a sum of £150,000 is left in trust. It is usual for the beneficiaries of the trust to include the couple's children, but grandchildren and other relatives may also be included. Arthur's will trust includes Enid as a potential beneficiary, while Enid's includes Arthur. Thus, on the first death, a sum of £150,000, which is within the inheritance tax 'nil rate band', is handed on to the next generation, and the surviving spouse now has less assets. When the surviving spouse dies there will be £150,000 less assets, and at a 40% rate of inheritance tax, this produces a £60,000 tax saving. The surviving spouse may be supported by distributions from the trust before his or her death if these are necessary.

You may not want to make lifetime gifts because you have doubts about whether the recipient will make good use of them. Where the intended recipient is a minor, it can be a good idea to make a lifetime gift to an accumulation and maintenance trust. Such trusts are virtually exempt from inheritance tax, and provided you live for seven years after making the gift, then gifts totalling £200,000 in any seven-year period will escape inheritance tax completely. The beneficiaries of such a trust must be entitled to receive the capital no later than age 25, and the trustees usually have the power to make distributions of capital to them earlier.

Edward and Jean are in their late 60s. They have substantial assets and want to give some to their two grandchildren, John and Helen. Edward makes a gift of £50,000 into a trust for John's benefit and Jean makes a gift of £50,000 into a trust for Helen's benefit. Neither Edward nor Jean have made any previous lifetime gifts, and since these gifts are within each individual's £200,000 nil-rate band, there will be no inheritance tax provided both Edward and Jean survive for another seven years. The income from the investments within the trust and the capital gains will be taxable, but there will be no inheritance tax charge when the assets are distributed to John and Helen.

Verdict: The greater the value of your assets, the more likely it is that establishing trusts will help you to reduce the potential inheritance tax bill on your death.

Offshore Tax Havens

Tax havens are where rich people park their money to avoid paying tax. This is the popular view and, as far as UK residents are concerned, it is almost completely false. Unless you emigrate and cease to be a resident of the UK, you are required by law to declare all your income from everywhere in the world and pay tax on it. Some rich people do emigrate to avoid having to do this – some countries have a less stringent attitude and only require you to pay tax on the money you bring into the country. In fact the UK has this more generous attitude to foreigners who are not permanently resident in the UK. It is only UK citizens who get the more brutal treatment.

So you cannot simply take a bag of cash to a sunny island with secretive banks and hope to escape tax. You may do so, but you may instead become the subject of an Inland Revenue investigation, which would turn your entire financial life upside down and you could end up either making a large agreed payment of back taxes (plus interest) or being prosecuted and then paying the back taxes plus a large fine.

But there are legitimate ways of using tax havens: various investments operated from tax havens can delay, reduce or even eliminate some of the UK taxes you would otherwise pay.

Investing through tax havens

Investment funds and bank accounts in places such as the Channel Islands, the Isle of Man, Bermuda and Luxembourg are not only tax-free themselves but are not required to deduct any tax from any interest or dividends they pay you. So it is relatively easy to defer the payment of UK income tax on interest. All you need is a fund based in a tax haven that receives its income gross, deducts no tax, and accumulates all this interest rather than paying it out to you. Since you receive no interest, you pay no tax. With this type of investment, known as an accumulator fund, when you cash in your investment, you pay income tax on the gain you have made on the shares or units in the fund.

These 'roll-up' or accumulator funds allow you to earn interest, and though the compounding effect will be negligible over a short period, it can make a useful difference to your returns over a longer period, even assuming you end up paying all the tax you would have done if you had received the interest as you went along. But if your income falls in the future – say after retirement – and your tax rate also falls from 40% to 20%, then use of these roll-up funds can enable you to make a 20% tax savings on all your interest accumulated over a period of years. And if you have no income when you encash your shares, you may escape tax on your accumulated interest altogether – as in the case of a married woman who is taking a career break while she brings up her young children.

Note that for UK residents, it does not usually make sense to accumulate capital gains in this way. All the gains from accumulator funds are taxable as income, whereas with normal capital gains, the first £6,300 a year is tax-free. So the use of these accumulator funds is effectively limited to funds that pay interest, either deposit-based funds or funds investing in fixed interest securities.

For UK residents, there is little to be gained by investing in offshore funds which themselves invest in shares. The fund itself may be in a tax haven and pay no tax, but most countries levy a withholding tax on dividends, so the fund will not receive the full dividend in the first place. The UK, for example, deducts 20% tax from all dividends. This can be offset by EU residents (and by residents of other countries which have tax treaties with the UK) against their local taxes, and if these are lower they can claim back the difference. A fund in a tax haven cannot normally claim back the withholding tax that has been deducted from its income, so as regards dividend income, a UK resident is usually better off investing in a domestic unit or investment trust than in an offshore fund.

As regards capital gains tax, there is no advantage for a UK resident in investing in offshore funds. With the exception of accumulator funds, these are treated in the same way for capital gains tax as domestic funds like unit trusts. When you sell your units or shares, your gain will be subject to capital gains tax in the normal way (though gains within the annual exemption escape tax).

Verdict: Apart from accumulator funds, few offshore funds offer UK investors any tax advantage. In most cases, the charges on such funds are also higher than on UK unit or investment trusts.

A life offshore

There is another category of offshore fund whose tax treatment for UK residents is far more complex but also potentially more useful: offshore life assurance policies. A number of insurers offer lump sum investments in the form of life assurance policies through companies located in the Channel Islands or the Isle of Man. As with other offshore funds, the funds themselves pay no tax on their investment income or gains, nor is any tax deducted from any payments the insurers make to you as a policyholder. These funds do suffer witholding taxes on dividends, however.

Within the life assurance policy you may have a large range of different funds to choose from, so that you can switch your money around from one type of investment to another whenever you wish. If you did this in normal investments like shares or unit or investment trusts, each sale would crystallize a gain which would be potentially subject to capital gains tax. But switches within an assurance policy are not assessable for capital gains tax. So if your annual gains are large enough, you can use this method to defer or avoid paying capital gains tax on your profits.

Lump sum life assurance policies are subject to special tax rules in the UK. You are allowed to withdraw a sum equal to your initial investment over a 20-year period without incurring any UK tax. The actual amount you can withdraw will depend on when you start to take such withdrawals. For example, if you start in the first year the maximum rate will be 5% a year ($20 \times 5\% = 100\%$), but if you start in the 10th year then the maximum rate would be 10% ($10\% \times 10 = 100\%$). This rule enables you to draw an 'income' from your investment: whether it is a genuine income – generated purely as income by the investments within the policy – will depend on the types of investments you have chosen.

If and when you cash in the policy, then UK income tax becomes payable on the whole gain. To determine the rate of tax that will apply, the gain is spread over the number of years the investment has been held. If you had held it for ten years and made a £20,000 profit, then £2,000 would be the annual gain and this amount would be added to your income in the year of encashment. The rate of tax on this extra slice of your income would then be applied to the whole gain. Note that there is one big difference between this tax regime and that for lump sum UK life policies: with UK policies, any gain is subject only to higher-rate tax, because UK life companies themselves pay tax at 20%, but gains on offshore policies are subject to both the standard-rate and higher-rate tax of income tax.

The overall situation of offshore life policies as regards income tax is therefore not very favourable, but there are ways of using them that enable you to avoid tax. Under UK legislation, if such a policy is placed within a trust, its original owner dies, and the trustees do not encash the policy until the tax year after the original owner's death, then under the quaintly named 'dead settlor' provision the gains accumulated within the policy escape both income tax and capital gains tax. This is because, in such cases, the income tax charge due on the accumulated gain on the policy's encashment is calculated by reference to the income tax rate of the original owner who transferred it into the trust (technically the settlor). The latest time when such a tax charge could be pinned on the settlor is the fiscal year in which he or she died: after this, there is no one to attach the tax charge to, so the gain built into the policy escapes tax-free, whether or not the policy is encashed. Effectively, then, such a policy can enable you to accumulate tax-free income and capital gains over a period of years up to your death, after which your spouse (as beneficiary of a trust) can encash it, also tax-free. And if instead of just being for the benefit of your spouse, the trust is a discretionary one where he or she has no automatic right to benefit, then the capital within the policy will also escape inheritance tax on your spouse's death.

Offshore life policies may be purchased by one spouse, and left to the other spouse under a will trust. They may also be held as investments within other types of trust. Here too they can have advantages, because with many offshore policies it is possible to add new lives assured to the policy, thus ensuring that the policy never needs to be encashed through the death of the person assured. So long as no withdrawals are made, the tax charge that would (under current UK legislation) occur on encashment can be deferred almost indefinitely.

Verdict: Investing through offshore life assurance policies can enable you to avoid income tax, capital gains tax and inheritance tax. But you need to enter complex and inflexible arrangements, which are potentially vulnerable to new anti-avoidance legislation in the future, and the costs can be high.

Unquoted Shares

The last few years have seen the extension of various tax concessions to shares in small companies. So long as these shares are not quoted on the Stock Exchange, they count as 'unquoted', which qualifies them for a variety of reliefs. Such shares include those listed on the Alternative Investment Market (AIM) established in 1995.

Company shares as a tax shelter

You can defer the tax payable on a capital gain you have already made (regardless of what type of asset the gain was made from) by reinvesting a sum equal to the gain in qualifying shares. So if you had made a taxable gain (after indexation and after deducting your £6,300 annual exemption) of £20,000 and invested this sum in qualifying shares, then the gains tax would not be payable until the new shares were sold: and if you at that point bought more qualifying shares, the tax on the original gain could be further postponed. This roll-over reinvestment relief alone should not prompt you to buy shares in the smaller and riskier companies that are listed on AIM. However, it appears likely that the range of shares listed on AIM will provide worthwhile opportunities, and if you are interested in the higher-risk, higher-reward sector of stock market investment then this is worth considering.

A further capital gains tax concession also applies to these shares. If you have a gain on them, you may elect to hold over the gain when you give them to another person. In normal circumstances, the only person to whom you can give assets without being regarded as having made a disposal which could crystallize a capital gains tax liability is your legal spouse. But unquoted shares (again including AIM shares) qualify for this 'holdover relief for gifts of business assets'.

Henry owns shares which cost him £10,000 but are now worth £50,000. He makes a gift of these shares to his grandson James. No capital gains tax is payable because Henry elects for holdover relief.

James is regarded as having acquired the shares for the original cost of £10,000 and is potentially liable to capital gains tax on his sale of the shares; but he could sell them in stages year by year, making use of his annual £6,300 exemption, and thus avoid paying any tax.

Unquoted shares – again including those listed on AIM – may also count as business assets in terms of inheritance tax, and are granted 100% relief from inheritance tax. If you have a large amount of capital invested in shares, then transfer of capital from shares listed on the Stock Exchange to those listed on AIM could yield substantial savings in inheritance tax.

If you make a loss on investment in an unquoted share (again including AIM shares), then provided you subscribed for the shares in the first place (and did not purchase them through the market from another shareholder), then you may offset the loss against your income in the year in which you dispose of the shares.

Verdict: Unquoted shares have a large package of tax concessions and if you benefit from several of them the tax savings can be very substantial. But again it must be emphasized that AIM shares and other unquoted shares are high-risk investments. Unless you are prepared to incur high risks, you should not be swayed by these tax concessions into investing in such risky assets.

9 ‖ *Avoiding Tax Traps*

If you save or invest in tax-exempt schemes, then you will certainly avoid paying tax you otherwise would have paid, and will improve the return you get on your money. But if this is all you do, you may still end up paying more tax than you need, because the tax system contains a number of tax traps – situations where you are forced to pay tax which, with a little care, can be avoided.

The Age Allowance Trap

One of these traps lies in wait for many people over the age of 65, who are entitled to age allowances. These are additional personal allowances against income tax, as listed in Table 17. The age allowances are in addition to the normal personal allowances (also listed in Table 17). But there is an income limit (£15,200 for 1996–97) and if your income exceeds this, then the age allowances are reduced at a rate of £1 for each £2 of excess income, until they are completely extinguished. This procedure applies only to the extra age allowances listed in the table and not to the normal personal allowances.

The income limit is your total gross income from all sources. The main categories of income that are excluded are: income from any tax-exempt schemes such as TESSAs or PEPs; the capital content of any regular payments you receive from lifetime or temporary annuities; and any withdrawals from lump sum life insurance investments that are within the normal allowance rules (in the case of guaranteed income bonds this will normally be 5% a year). Permitted deductions in arriving at the total income are any tax-deductible interest payments, pension plan contributions, charitable covenant payments and some categories of maintenance payments.

Table 17: Age allowances for 1995–96 and 1996–97

	Tax year 1995–96	Tax year 1996–97
Normal personal allowance	£3,525	£3,765
Normal married couples allowance*	£1,720	£1,790
Extra allowances for those aged 65–74		
Additional personal allowance	£1,105	£1,145
Additional married couples allowance*	£1,275	£1,325
Extra allowances for those aged over 75		
Additional personal allowance	£1,275	£1,325
Additional married couples allowance*	£1,315	£1,365
Income limit for age allowances	£14,600	£15,200

* These allowances are not offset against taxable income in the same way as personal allowances. Instead they are converted into tax credits at a rate of 15%.

When your personal income exceeds the income limit, the excess income is always used first to restrict the personal allowance. Only after this has been used up is any excess income used to reduce the married couples allowance.

The effect of having income in excess of the threshold is to create a marginal tax rate of 30% on a band of investment income of up to £2,650. This arises because when you have an additional, say, £20 of excess income, you lose £10 of age allowance. So you pay tax at 20% on the £20 (£4 in tax) but you also have £10 more taxable income because your allowance is reduced, so you pay an extra £2 in tax, making £6 in tax on £20 of income or 30%.

On top of this there is, for married men, a band of income of up to £2,730 on which the marginal tax rate will be 27.5%. This arises because after the personal allowance has been reduced to the normal level of £3,765, any additional income above the £15,200 threshold is used to reduce the married couples allowance from its higher, age allowance, level down to the normal level of £1,790.

So, for a married man aged over 75, for example, the effect of having £20 extra investment income above £17,850 (the level at which the personal allowance has been reduced to the normal level) is to pay £4 extra tax on the £20 of income and to have the tax credit from the married couples allowance reduced by £1.50 (15% of £10). This makes a total tax bill of £5.50 on £20 or 27.5%.

If, as a married person, you have a large pension income, in excess of £15,200, then there is nothing you can do to avoid the loss of age allowance. But if you have investment income that is pushing your total income over the income limit, then you may be able to rearrange your investments to avoid the loss of some or all of the allowance.

Richard and Elsie are both aged 66. Richard has pension income (the State pension and an occupational pension) of £13,300. He also has gross investment income of £4,190 a year, so his total income is £17,490. He therefore loses all the additional age allowance and is restricted to the normal personal allowance of £3,765. Elsie has pension income of £9,000 and investment income of £2,000, some of it from investments held jointly with Richard, like the building society account. Now, if Richard transfers to Elsie the ownership of sufficient investments to reduce his total income to £15,200, then he will get his age allowance in full. Her total income will rise from £11,000 to £13,290, so she will also still be entitled to her full age allowance. Note that both Richard and Elsie were and are standard-rate taxpayers. By changing the ownership of investments Richard will receive his full personal age allowance of £1,145 (saving £229 in tax).

Accumulating Capital Gains

The annual exemption for capital gains tax is relatively generous at £6,300. But many people end up paying capital gains tax because they do not make use of the exemption. Instead they accumulate gains over a period of years and then, when they sell their assets, face a gains tax bill. The best way to avoid this is to sell investments on an annual basis to take advantage of the exemption. This does not mean you have to get rid of the investment in question. With shares, unit and investment trusts, you can follow the procedure known as 'bed-and-breakfasting'; you sell the asset and buy it back again a few days later. The price at which you buy it back again is the new acquisition cost for any future capital gains tax calculation. So you take a capital gain within your annual exemption and increase the cost base of the asset, thus reducing any possible future capital gains tax liability. The cost of the exercise is around 2% of the value of the investments.

Bed-and-breakfasting can help to avoid piling up taxable gains. But there are also other ways you can prevent capital gains tax from taking too much of your profit.

David has made a gain of £15,000 after indexation and after allowing for the annual exemption. The rate of capital gains tax is determined by adding the gain to taxable income in the year when the gain is made so, adding the gain to his gross income of £25,000, this will result in capital gains tax at 40% on most of the gain. But David is self-employed and has unused relief for pension contributions of £15,000. By investing £15,000 in a pension plan he will reduce his taxable income to £10,000. When the gain is added to his income, the rate of capital gains tax on most of the gain will be 24%, with a tax saving of about £1,500.

Redistribution of assets between husband and wife can also cut capital gains tax bills. When you make such a transfer, the person taking over the asset is regarded as having acquired it at the same cost as the original owner. So if either husband or wife owns an asset on which they will incur a taxable capital gain, it is always worth considering if a transfer of all or part of the asset to the spouse will result in a lower tax bill.

Jenny inherited a flat from her mother 10 years ago and now wants to sell it. The value has grown from £60,000 when she inherited it to

£100,000, so there will be a large liability to capital gains tax, and since Jenny's income is £20,000, most of the gain will be taxed at 40%. However Jenny can transfer a half share in the ownership of the property to her husband Ian. Then, when they sell the property, they will benefit from two annual exemptions of £6,300 instead of one, saving over £2,300 in tax. In addition to this, since Ian's income is about £15,000, the first part of his gain will bear tax at 24%, so there will be an extra tax saving of about £1,500.

Tax gain or tax loss

One fact has become apparent to some people who have invested in self-select PEPs: you may escape capital gains tax on any profits you make in a PEP, but you also lose the option of setting any capital loss against other profits you may make. Losses incurred within a PEP cannot be offset against profits on other investments.

You therefore need to think carefully about which investments to place inside your PEP. Of course, the biggest tax advantage you gain from PEPs is the exemption from income tax, since this produces an immediate tax saving, whereas any saving in capital gains tax is, at the point when you buy an investment, hypothetical. If you own a variety of investments, then, and do not expect to make regular gains in excess of your annual exemption, it makes more sense to place within PEPs first those investments that produce a higher income and, second, those with the lower risk. The higher-risk investments, while likely to produce larger gains, may also produce losses and in practice you may well have both gains and losses on different investments, in which case one can be offset against the other and you may pay no tax.

The Tax-saving Trap

The biggest tax trap of all is to make a decision solely on the grounds of an immediate or expected saving in tax. The right way to set about making investment or saving decisions is to think about what type of assets you want to buy, and only after you have made this strategic decision to try to arrange the ownership of these investments in the way that involves the payment of the least possible tax. Aspects you will have to consider include not just the availability of tax shelters like PEPs, pension plans and TESSAs but also, for married couples, the ownership of investments.

Making tax-led investment decisions has probably caused investors far more losses than it has made them profits over the years. A variety of 'tax shelters' in the 1970s, such as partnerships investing in oil wells, produced a large crop of disasters, as did the Business Expansion Scheme and Property Enterprise Trusts in the 1980s.

People seem to get fixated on the tax savings and forget that they are investing their money in something. Often, when a tax concession is attached to it, this something is more risky than run-of-the-mill investments, and should therefore require far more, rather than less, careful analysis and consideration. On top of that, many tax shelter schemes have in the past breached another cardinal rule of the investment professionals by requiring the investment of over 10% of free capital in order to achieve the tax savings. In general, professional investors consider investment of over 10% of your free capital in any single investment as a very high-risk procedure regardless of how good the investment may appear to be.

The moral is clear: tax should always take second place. The investment aspect should always come first. Only invest in assets you are confident will produce the return you are looking for and, most important, with a level of risk which you understand and accept. Tax savings that reduce the losses incurred on a bad investment are cold comfort, but tax savings added to a good investment are the icing on the cake.

10 ‖ *How to Select the Best Tax-free Savings Plans and Investments*

There are far too many financial products available in the UK. Virtually every financial organization has launched its own range of plans, usually declaring that it has done so 'in order to serve the needs of its customers'. But none of these organizations are charities and the vast majority of these plans are mediocre or downright poor value for money.

Most readers will be customers of several financial organizations – banks, building societies and life assurance companies, for example. None of these have any automatic right to your business. Any one organization will rarely offer good value for money across its whole product range, so even if you have bought one good-value product from an assurance company, for example, don't assume that this company's PEP will also be good value. There are definite financial gains to be made by shopping around for the best buy.

First let us define 'good value'. In relation to saving and investment plans, good value has two principal components:

- **Costs and charges.** These vary greatly from plan to plan, and the effect of these variations on the net return you get from your money is spelt out below.
- **Product features.** It is very rare for any plan to have genuinely unique features, but some plans will offer more flexibility than others, for example. Some investment managers do have a much better track record of past performance than others, and some organizations provide a better after-sales service than others.

Balancing Costs, Features and Past Performance

You need to consider costs and features together. Usually, the more flexible a plan, the higher its charges, because the managers have to undertake that much more administration. So if you are considering, say, a PEP for regular savings, you need to be clear about how much flexibility you really need. If you are confident that you can stick to a straightforward £500 a month saving, you may not need a plan that allows you to stop, start, and vary your payments. If you can find a plan that incorporates such features at no extra cost, fine, but there is no point in paying higher charges for unnecessary features.

The most difficult question in choosing saving and investment plans is how much weight to give to investment managers' past performance records. Sales and marketing executives often assert, quite correctly, that if their investment managers earn a very small extra annual return on top of the market average, this will compensate for their plan's higher charges. And they point to the fact that their investment managers have earned such high returns in the past to justify their claim that they are likely to do so in the future. Many organizations use this argument to justify above-average charges on their plans.

In practice, a great deal of academic research into investment performance has found no statistically significant evidence that investment managers do or can consistently produce above-average results year after year. In every year, a few investment managers do much better than the mass of their competitors. But the following year, it will not be the first year's winners but a different set of investment managers who produce the best performance, and there is a tendency for returns to 'regress towards the mean' – in other words for all investment managers' returns to gradually drift towards the average over time.

There are a few apparent exceptions: investment organizations which have produced consistently good results over long periods of time. The academics compare this to the situation of 1,000 people tossing coins. After 100 tosses, they say, the fact that one person has thrown heads 100 times in a row does not make him more likely to throw heads next time: the odds remain 50–50. If you have enough people tossing coins, there are sure to be one or two who throw heads many times in succession, but these are not coin-tossing geniuses: they are the products of a normal statistical distribution of results in a random process.

The implications of this for plan selection are that you should adopt a double-pronged selection method. It is worth avoiding plans whose managers have produced worse than average investment performance in the past. You do not want to be caught by a statistical freak and invest in a plan that produces bad results 10 years in a row. It is also worth favouring plans whose managers have produced good past results, but not if this means paying above-average charges. And on the whole, evidence of a steady record of respectable performance in the past is preferable to a mixed record of good years alternating with bad. Also worth avoiding are funds and managers that have recently produced spectacularly good results: the evidence is that exceptionally good results are usually followed by poor ones.

Measuring investment performance

Past investment performance is largely about numbers. And managers usually display the best set of numbers they can. So if you really want objective comparisons between different investment managers and the funds they manage, you will need to turn to independent sources such as the monthly journals that publish performance statistics, or to an independent financial adviser who subscribes to one of the database services providing all the data for analysis on a desktop computer.

One pitfall snares many investors: the phenomenon of the 'false boost'. Imagine a fund which performs dismally for two years, and so does worse than most of its rivals. Then, under threat of the sack, the investment manager picks a few really risky shares which come good, soaring in value. The result is that over the last few months, this fund outpaces all its rivals. Worse still, if all you look at is the performance figures up to the present date, it looks as though it has outperformed its rivals over a period of two years. If a fund's most recent performance is good it can conceal a poor previous record. The only way to identify good performance that is consistent rather than flash-in-the-pan is to look at a series of period-to-period figures. So instead of looking just at performance over different periods of time up to, say, December 1995, you would look at the performance in calendar 1995, calendar 1994, and calendar 1993 as well.

Fund managers do not, of course, publish figures in this form. The only way you can get hold of them is by going to a library and looking them up in back issues of a magazine (like *Money Management* or *Money Observer*) that regularly publishes the data. But you can also get such data from an adviser who uses one of the database services (Micropal and Hindsight).

Professional analysts of fund performance do not give funds much credit for being the best in their sector over one period of time. What they tend to ask is whether the fund has consistently been in the top 25% of similar funds over different periods of time measured up to different end-dates. Once you look at the data in this way, you find there are very few funds in any sectors which have consistently been in the top 25% over a majority of the periods measured. There is some evidence that selecting the funds which score best on this basis produces measurably better results than selecting funds at random.

The average results of investing £1,000 and saving £100 per month over various periods in different types of fund are shown in Table 18. For details of how to get up-to-date figures, see Appendix I (page 149). Note the wide range of variation in the encashment values depending on the end-date at which the results are measured. The encashment values of all unit funds vary directly with the movement of the relevant markets, so never take cash-in values calculated to one point in time as a reliable guide to past performance. An average of cash-in results over several periods, like those used in the table, is a more reliable guide to future results.

Table 18(a): Results of investing £100 per month

Type of fund	Period in years			
	5	10	15	20
Unit Trusts				
UK equity growth				
to 1st December 1995	£8,537	£21,134	£59,567	£148,360
to 1st July 1992	£6,899	£23,018	£66,537	£158,353
to 1st July 1990	£7,987	£31,908	£86,807	N/A
UK equity income				
to 1st December 1995	£8,503	£22,779	£73,046	£194,332
to 1st July 1992	£7,055	£27,262	£82,272	£201,026
to 1st July 1990	£8,759	£39,740	£114,195	N/A
International balanced				
to 1st December 1995	£8,116	£21,674	£78,944	N/A
to 1st July 1992	£7,074	£30,767	N/A	N/A
to 1st July 1990	£8,705	£39,584	N/A	N/A
North America				
to 1st December 1995	£9,791	£25,706	£51,522	£108,595
to 1st July 1992	£7,227	£17,285	£42,469	£95,053
to 1st July 1990	£7,496	£21,602	£51,482	N/A
Europe				
to 1st December 1995	£8,824	£22,194	£66,760	£186,632
to 1st July 1992	£7,030	£24,483	£76,043	£173,001
to 1st July 1990	£9,758	£44,746	£125,129	£332,178
Japan				
to 1st December 1995	£7,058	£15,805	£43,184	£119,342
to 1st July 1992	£4,482	£15,560	£46,166	£104,118
to 1st July 1990	£9,048	£35,279	£109,205	N/A
Far East (excl. Japan)				
to 1st December 1995	£9,821	£32,442	£70,754	N/A
to 1st July 1992	£9,153	£24,378	N/A	N/A
to 1st July 1990	£9,842	£33,553	N/A	N/A

UK smaller companies

to 1st December 1995	£8,772	£20,312	£52,303	£144,556
to 1st July 1992	£6,282	£21,204	£61,385	£170,359
to 1st July 1990	£7,331	£29,288	£88,605	N/A

Unitized personal pension funds

UK equity

to 1st December 1995	£8,376	£21,438	£56,593	£139,966
to 1st July 1992	£7,003	£23,396	£64,473	£132,402
to 1st July 1990	£8,294	£31,026	£84,860	N/A

International

to 1st December 1995	£8,408	£20,916	£49,119	N/A
to 1st July 1992	£6,537	£19,073	N/A	N/A
to 1st July 1990	£7,870	£24,694	N/A	N/A

Managed (3-way)

to 1st December 1995	£8,171	£20,949	£51,571	£118,781
to 1st July 1992	£7,029	£21,246	£56,069	£107,596
to 1st July 1990	£8,069	£27,332	£66,165	N/A

Investment trusts

International general

to 1st December 1995	£9,053	£26,976	£84,498	£246,787
to 1st July 1992	£8,098	£28,090	£90,891	N/A
to 1st July 1990	£9,093	£38,311	£112,857	N/A

UK General

to 1st December 1995	£9,489	£26,216	£77,681	£222,792
to 1st July 1992	£7,326	£26,071	£86,829	N/A
to 1st July 1990	£8,575	£35,411	£121,903	N/A

UK income growth

to 1st December 1995	£8,985	£26,515	£94,517	£289,270
to 1st July 1992	£8,177	£33,384	£117,300	N/A
to 1st July 1990	£9,478	£45,510	£144,837	N/A

Europe

to 1st December 1995	£8,457	£22,220	£63,499	£163,947
to 1st July 1992	£6,813	£22,076	£65,637	N/A
to 1st July 1990	£10,405	£43,401	£119,603	N/A

Table 18(b): Results from an initial investment of £1,000

Type of fund	Period in years			
	5	10	15	20
Unit Trusts				
UK equity growth				
to 1st December 1995	£2,023	£3,282	£9,181	£21,105
to 1st July 1992	£1,089	£5,064	£11,008	£11,371
to 1st July 1990	£2,288	£6,193	£13,304	N/A
UK equity income				
to 1 December 1995	£1,997	£3,957	£13,174	£30,418
to 1st July 1992	£1,241	£6,580	£13,480	£18,525
to 1st July 1990	£2,642	£8,020	£21,333	N/A
International balanced				
to 1st December 1995	£1,937	£3,619	£13,580	N/A
to 1st July 1992	£1,243	£7,167	N/A	N/A
to 1st July 1990	£2,739	£8,013	N/A	N/A
North America				
to 1st December 1995	£2,983	£3,301	£6,818	£11,741
to 1st July 1992	£1,170	£3,288	£5,109	£6,028
to 1st July 1990	£1,444	£4,532	£5,612	N/A
Europe				
to 1st December 1995	£1,991	£3,614	£11,075	£24,180
to 1st July 1992	£1,237	£6,356	£12,010	£14,280
to 1st July 1990	£3,026	£8,710	£16,216	£40,776
Japan				
to 1st December 1995	£1,517	£2,966	£8,337	£17,581
to 1st July 1992	£ 836	£4,051	£6,500	£11,770
to 1st July 1990	£3,068	£8,716	£16,972	N/A
Far East (excl. Japan)				
to 1st December 1995	£3,287	£5,898	£11,260	N/A
to 1st July 1992	£1,545	£3,710	N/A	N/A
to 1st July 1990	£2,446	£6,913	N/A	N/A
UK Smaller Companies				
to 1st December 1995	£2,183	£3,296	£8,514	£25,477
to 1st July 1992	£ 894	£4,634	£11,484	£13,745
to 1st July 1990	£2,223	£5,980	£18,125	N/A

Unitized personal pension funds

UK equity

to 1st December 1995	£1,962	£3,377	£8,588	£19,136
to 1st July 1992	£1,155	£4,947	£10,324	£10,776
to 1st July 1990	£2,339	£6,090	£13,276	N/A

International

to 1st December 1995	£2,141	£3,043	£7,413	N/A
to 1st July 1992	£1,063	£4,236	N/A	N/A
to 1st July 1990	£1,967	£4,746	N/A	N/A

Managed (3-way)

to 1st December 1995	£1,900	£3,092	£7,411	£15,752
to 1st July 1992	£1,234	£4,016	£8,172	£7,631
to 1st July 1990	£2,056	£4,931	£9,250	N/A

Investment trusts

International general

to 1st December 1995	£2,489	£4,567	£14,694	£32,659
to 1st July 1992	£1,397	£6,801	£15,778	N/A
to 1st July 1990	£2,476	£8,388	£15,790	N/A

UK General

to 1st December 1995	£2,366	£4,314	£12,999	£38,041
to 1st July 1992	£1,226	£6,125	£16,986	N/A
to 1st July 1990	£2,345	£7,626	£22,025	N/A

UK income growth

to 1st December 1995	£2,334	£4,686	£17,949	£41,700
to 1st July 1992	£1,462	£8,924	£21,135	N/A
to 1st July 1990	£2,807	£10,675	£22,333	N/A

Europe

to 1st December 1995	£1,753	£3,344	£9,705	£18,698
to 1st July 1992	£1,138	£5,509	£11,344	N/A
to 1st July 1990	£2,746	£9,106	£14,031	N/A

All figures are calculated offer-to-offer price with gross income reinvested and are the averages for all funds in the relevant sector.
Source: Micropal

The effect of charges

New regulations on disclosure of charges which came into effect in 1995 mean that you can now compare the charges made by different plans. This is important, because the methods of charging vary, and it is not at all obvious at first sight whether you will end up with a bigger payout if you pay 5% on the amounts you save plus 1% a year on the value of your plan, or 3.5% on your subscriptions plus 1.25% a year.

Disclosure does not apply to investments or plans offering a straightforward rate of interest, such as TESSAs or National Savings Certificates. Here you can directly compare one interest rate with another so you do not need to know about costs and charges. Disclosure does apply to most investment products. These include all life assurance and friendly society plans that acquire a maturity or encashment value, all individual pension plans, all unit trusts, all PEPs and all offshore funds and life assurance policies licensed for marketing in the UK.

Before disclosure was introduced, plan promoters benefited from complex charging structures: the more complex the method of charging, the more difficult it was for anyone to work out the effects. However, all charges and costs now have to be reflected in the information required by the disclosure regulations; nothing can be hidden. In time, therefore, there may be a trend to simpler charging structures.

The most important set of numbers in the disclosure documents (received on request from any plan manager) is the table of encashment values. Assuming a given rate of return on your money, this shows how much you would get at various points in time if you cashed in your plan after all charges had been deducted. Typically, plans which produce the best early encashment values – during the first few years – will not produce the best payouts after long periods such as 20 years.

In choosing a saving plan or investment fund it is therefore logical to look first of all for the one which produces the highest payout at the end of your chosen savings period, assuming the same annual growth rate is achieved. But if you think you may well actually encash the plan earlier, then you would be wise to select the plan that has higher encashment values in the earlier years, even if this means making a slightly smaller profit if you do maintain the plan for the full intended term.

Disclosure documents for pension and life insurance plans also include two columns – one showing the actual total charges deducted over a period of years and the other showing the effect of these deductions. This last column could be misleading, stating as it does the difference between the amount you could have got if your money had been invested at the given gross annual rate of return with no charges and the actual amount of the expected payout after charges. This comparison with a no-charge plan is misleading because it simply is not possible to save or invest without paying any charges.

Reduction in yield

Of more relevance is the disclosure of the effect of charges on the rate of return. If the gross rate of return is 7.5% a year, the statement may show that charges reduce the return you can expect to 6% a year – in other words, the return will be reduced by 1.5% a year. This is called a 'Reduction in Yield' statement. Think of this as a fraction to put it into perspective: a reduction of 1.5% out of 7.5% is one fifth. Is it reasonable for a plan to take a fifth of the total return in charges? There is no simple answer to this, since the average charge varies with the type of plan, its term, and even with the amount you save or invest. The RIY will always be very high if you encash early and incur penalties for doing so.

However, for most long-term savings plans, Reductions in Yield should not be over a fifth, since the best-value plans levy charges of less than this. Poor-value plans can involve RIYs of a quarter or even more.

Commission

The payout figures in the disclosure documents are after deducting all costs and charges. These costs include any commissions payable to salesmen or agents. It is always the total cost figure that is relevant in terms of value-for-money comparisons, not the commission, which represents only a small proportion of the total cost. The amount of commission may be a relevant factor, however, because a reduction in the commission may increase a plan's payouts. In the case of independent financial advisers commissions are negotiable, so if you feel the amount is too high you may request a reduction. If the commission is reduced, then more of your money will be invested in the plan, and the effect of this 'commission rebate' should show up, in new disclosure documents, as higher payouts. Sales representatives of assurance companies, and representatives of banks and building societies, who also receive commission, are usually unable to improve their plan payouts by rebating commission in this way.

Commission is therefore a secondary consideration. Value for money shows up in the encashment values, and it is quite possible for Plan A, which pays a higher rate of commission than Plan B, to show higher future payouts than Plan B if the same growth rate is assumed. Different organizations have different methods of distributing and selling their products. Some of these involve payment of commission and some do not. For example, some companies sell direct to the customer through newspaper advertisements, they have no salesmen, so they make no commission payments, but the costs of the advertisements have to come out of the plan charges. It is important, then, not to assume that plans paying higher commissions are necessarily worse value for money. This is not always the case.

If you arrange your savings or investments through an adviser who charges fees, he or she will usually either select plans which pay no commissions, or will arrange commission rebates with plans that do. In both cases this will improve the value for money of the relevant plans. But here you need to take account of any fee you pay the adviser. When you get 'free' financial advice and pay commissions, the commissions are paying for the advice. So it is unrealistic to ignore the costs of advice when you pay fees instead.

Ideally, you should consider financial advice from two quite separate standpoints. Firstly, there is the generic advice or financial planning advice. This is based on knowledge of your personal circumstances and provides overall advice on how you can achieve your objectives. Secondly, there is advice on the selection of specific financial products, whether these are savings and investment plans, life assurance or health insurance.

Financial planning advice

The first type of financial advice – financial planning advice – should require extensive training, knowledge of all the aspects of personal taxation, the framework of insurance and assurance law and practice, and a sound understanding of investment, and should indeed be viewed as a professional skill similar to that possessed by lawyers or accountants (accountants, by the way, do not necessarily possess these personal financial planning skills). Unfortunately, only a minority of the salesmen employed by life assurance companies or by tied agents such as banks and building societies possess such knowledge and qualifications, though regulation in recent years has meant that standards are rising.

As regards independent financial advisers, standards also vary widely and while some have knowledge and training equivalent to that of professionals in other fields, many do not and are little more than product salesmen. Here too a recent drive by the industry's regulators is improving standards.

To sum up, you may obtain financial planning advice from salesmen employed by life assurers, from independent financial advisers remunerated by commission, or from independent advisers to whom you pay a fee.

Selection of financial products

The second type of advice – advice on the products you buy – is sharply divided between those who can give you independent advice on a wide range of products and those who cannot. Salesmen employed by a financial concern (such as a life assurance company), or by a tied agent (such as most building societies), may only advise you on that one company's financial products and are forbidden by law from advising you on other companies' products. Only independent advisers are permitted to advise on the whole range of products available on the market.

Independent advisers are often remunerated by commission from the companies whose products they sell to you. Since some products on the market do *not* pay commission, this must cast doubt on the impartiality of these advisers. Advisers who are paid by commissions rather than fees will occasionally advise you to buy products on which they earn no commissions, but on the whole – unsurprisingly – independent advisers remunerated by commissions do tend to recommend products of companies which pay them commissions. If you think of independent financial advisers as brokers, who can 'shop the market' for the best-value product, you will have a more realistic picture of their role.

In theory, independent advisers are bound by regulations under the Financial Services Act to put their client's interests first. But it is always possible to find some grounds for rejecting a particular product, so advisers who want to steer their clients from non-commission-paying to commission-paying products can almost always find reasons for doing so.

The situation is not as bad as it seems for two reasons. Firstly, most financial companies pay roughly equivalent commissions on similar products, so independent advisers do not normally have large incentives for persuading you to buy poor-value products. On the contrary, surveys regularly show that the products available through independent advisers are, on average, better value than those sold by life assurers through their sales forces or high street outlets. Secondly, regulation of independent advisers by the

Personal Investment Authority is fairly stringent, and those who breach the rules can be permanently barred from the industry.

By now you will have realized why disclosure is so important: for the first time, it gives you an objective measure of the value for money of recommended products. So when you are considering a major saving or investment decision, it is always worth getting advice from two different sources, and carefully comparing not only the features of the products recommended but the costs built into those products, as shown by their projected encashment values.

In recent years some independent financial advisers have taken to offering large commission rebates in an attempt to win new business. Several advertise regularly in newspapers offering big reductions in the initial commissions on purchases of PEPs or unit trusts. So if you are prepared to do your own research and make your own decisions, you can secure worthwhile cost savings that will improve the value for money of the products you buy.

Are You Protected?

Reading this book should ensure that you do not fall prey to over-enthusiastic salesmen offering dubious propositions for doubling your money overnight. But you will want to know what the position is if something does go horribly wrong. To what extent is your money protected?

The first point to make clear is that there is no protection against bad investment decisions. If you choose an Emerging Markets investment fund and its price crashes along with that of other funds in this sector, do not expect to get any compensation for your loss from anyone. And the same will usually apply if someone advises you to buy an Emerging Markets fund. Provided your circumstances, and your expressed attitude to risk justified such a recommendation at the time it was made (something every adviser is now required to establish and to record on file), then you cannot with hindsight claim the adviser should have known better or use a change in your circumstances to justify a claim that you should never have been advised to invest in such a fund in the first place.

The existing system of investor protection – termed 'self-regulation' under the Financial Services Act but in practice tending more and more to a system of policing-style regulation – is intended to protect investors against theft, dishonesty, fraud, incompetence and the financial failure of any advisory firm or savings or investment plan provider.

Protection against financial failure is covered, in the case of banks or building societies, to the extent of 90% of the first £20,000 of any individual's loss, i.e. a maximum of £18,000. Given the sums routinely deposited by individuals in banks and building societies, this level of protection is completely inadequate. This means you should exercise great care in the selection of institutions with which you deposit your money. Obviously the major high street banks and building societies are safe, but there are many smaller banks and deposit-taking companies which are not necessarily safe. Every year a certain number go bust and any individual who has deposited over £20,000 – as many have, lured by that extra percent or two of interest – loses out.

In the case of intermediaries such as financial advisers and stockbrokers, and investment institutions like unit trusts and Personal Equity Plan managers, a failure would entitle anyone who lost money as a result to claim up to £48,000 through the Investors Compensation Scheme, the industry-wide scheme run by the Personal Investment Authority. In the case of life assurance companies, the Policyholders Protection Act protects 90% of the benefits secured by the policies of any UK insurance or assurance company that fails.

Protection against fraud, theft, dishonesty and incompetence, whether by an adviser or investment manager, is also provided by the Investors Compensation Scheme. Access to such compensation is through a complaint to the relevant self-regulatory organization – in the case of most of the investments covered in this book, the Personal Investment Authority. But there are additional safeguards. One is the Ombudsmen – Pensions, Banking, Building Societies, Insurance and Investment. Each of them has the power to investigate complaints against any member company, usually in a relatively speedy and informal way, and to make judgements against them. Many investors have been compensated by companies for the consequences of inappropriate advice following Ombudsman judgements.

Specific investments also embody other protections. In the case of unit trusts, for example, there is an independent trustee company which holds all the trust's assets. It is therefore physically impossible for a unit trust manager to run off with the money; but even if a manager found a way of doing so, the trustee would be bound to compensate investors for their losses.

Unit trust managers, Personal Equity Plan managers, stockbrokers and independent financial advisers are all subject to prudential regulation under the Financial Services Act, which requires adequate reserves, vets the 'fitness' of individual directors and requires regular publication of independently audited financial accounts.

Personal pension funds run by insurance companies are covered by the Policholders Protection Act. Occupational pension funds – those run by employers – are not. The case of the late tycoon Robert Maxwell, and his looting of the *Daily Mirror* pension scheme, highlighted the need for improvements in security in this area. Some have been made but most experts believe determined fraudsters could still make off with pension fund assets. If you are a member of a pension scheme, read your annual statements and find out who the trustees of the pension scheme are. At least one trustee often represents the interests of employees.

By comparison with many other countries, the UK's financial services industry is well regulated, though the actual methods of regulation have been widely criticized in recent years on account of their excessive bureaucracy. And it is also worth pointing out that regulation is not free; nor is it paid for by the taxpayer. All the costs of regulation under the Financial Services Act are paid for by you and by everyone else who buys financial products, since all the regulators' charges – and the amounts paid out in compensation – are recovered from levies on the product providers.

Directory of Tax-Free Savings Schemes

Tax Exempt Special Savings Account (TESSA)

Eligibility: Age 18.
Term of scheme: Five years.
Minimum investment: £1 to £3,000, depending on scheme.
Maximum investment: For new schemes, a total of £9,000 over a five-year period. The maximum investment in the first year is £3,000, followed by a maximum of £1,800 in subsequent years. For reinvestments from existing accounts, the maximum initial and total investment is £9,000.
Tax concessions: No tax on interest.
Restrictions: Accounts may be in individual names only. All capital must remain invested until the fifth anniversary of commencement in order to retain tax concession.
Early encashment penalties: All interest becomes taxable.
Access to cash: Interest equal to gross interest less a notional deduction of income tax at 20% may be withdrawn without losing tax concession. Capital may be withdrawn, subject to agreed notice provisions.
Scheme operators: Banks and building societies.
Charges and costs: Transfer charges, normally £15–£25.

National Savings Certificates

Eligibility: Age 18; adults may invest 'under trust' on behalf of minors.
Term of scheme: Five years.
Minimum investment: £100.

Maximum investment: Varies with each issue. Normally £5,000 or £10,000.

Tax concessions: No tax on accumulated interest on encashment.

Restrictions: None.

Early encashment penalties: Reduction in the interest rate as compared with the rate payable on an investment held for the full term.

Access to cash: At any time.

Scheme operators: Department for National Savings.

Charges and costs: None.

Personal Equity Plan (PEP)

Eligibility: Minimum age 18. Must be a UK resident.

Term of scheme: Unspecified.

Minimum investment: Depends on scheme operators: £50 per month to £6,000.

Maximum investment: General PEPs: £6,000 in any fiscal year. Single Company PEPs: £3,000 in any fiscal year.

Tax concessions: * No income tax on dividends * No capital gains tax on gains * No tax on withdrawals at any time.

Restrictions: Plans in individual names only.

Early encashment penalties: No tax penalties. Cost penalties may be levied by scheme operators.

Access to cash: At any time.

Scheme operators: Investment management companies, banks and building societies.

Charges and costs: Depends on scheme operator: initial charges on investments: 0.5–5%; annual charges on fund values: 0.5–1.5%.

Additional Voluntary Contribution Scheme (AVC)

Eligibility: Employees who are members of occupational pension schemes.

Term of scheme: Up to retirement.

Minimum investment: Depends on scheme operators: £20–£100 per month.

Maximum investment: Total personal contributions to occupational pension scheme plus AVC together must not exceed 15% of earnings.

Tax concessions: * Income tax relief at the individual's highest marginal rate on contributions to the scheme * No income tax or capital gains tax on investments within the scheme * No tax at maturity of scheme.

Restrictions: Accumulated fund must be used to provide lifetime income through purchase of an annuity between ages 50 and 75.

Early encashment penalties: No encashment is permitted.

Access to cash: None.

Scheme operators: Employing company; insurance companies.

Charges and costs: Company schemes: under 1% annually; free-standing schemes: initial charges on subscriptions 1–5%; annual charges on fund values 1–1.5%.

Personal Pension Plan

Eligibility: Self-employed or employees who are not members of occupational pension schemes. Minimum age 18.

Term of scheme: Up to retirement.

Minimum investment: Depends on scheme operator: £50 per month to £10,000.

Maximum investment: A percentage of qualifying earnings that depends on age (see table on page 57).

Tax concessions: * Tax relief on contributions at highest marginal income tax rate * No income tax or capital gains tax on investments within the scheme * Up to 25% of the accumulated fund may be taken as tax-free cash at retirement.

Restrictions: Other than the 25% tax-free cash, the accumulated fund must be used to provide lifetime pension income on retirement between the ages of 50 and 75.

Early encashment penalties: No encashment is permitted.

Access to cash: Only to 25% of accumulated fund at retirement.
Scheme operators: Insurance companies, investment management companies.
Charges and costs: Depends on scheme operator; considerable variations in complex charging systems.

Friendly Society Savings Plan

Eligibility: Age 18 for normal plans; plans may be taken out in the names of minors.
Term of scheme: 10 years.
Minimum investment: £9 per month.
Maximum investment: £25 per month.
Tax concessions: * No income tax or capital gains tax on investments within the scheme * No tax is payable at maturity.
Restrictions: Plans must be continued for 10 years from inception to qualify for the tax concessions.
Early encashment penalties: Encashment value not exempt from tax. Cost penalties may be levied by scheme operators.
Access to cash: On early surrender subject to penalties.
Schemes operators: Tax-exempt friendly societies.
Charges and costs: Depends on scheme operator; considerable variations in complex charging systems.

Venture Capital Trust (VCT)

Eligibility: UK residents aged 18 and over.
Term of scheme: Five years.
Minimum investment: Depends on scheme operator.
Maximum investment: £100,000 in any fiscal year.
Tax concessions: * Income tax relief at a maximum of 20% on initial subscriptions for shares * No income tax on dividends paid by the VCT * No income tax or capital gains tax on investments held within the scheme * Deferral of capital gains tax payable on previous gains.

Restrictions: Shares must be held for at least five years. Trusts must meet the 'qualifying' criteria each year.

Early encashment penalties: * Clawback of initial income tax relief on subscription for shares * Crystallization of any capital gains tax that was deferred by making the investment * Any capital gain is potentially subject to capital gains tax.

Access to cash: Through sale of shares on the Stock Exchange.

Scheme operators: Investment management companies.

Charges and costs: Depends on scheme operators: costs on initial subscription 3–6%; annual charges on fund values 1–3%.

Enterprise Investment Scheme (EIS)

Eligibility: UK residents aged over 18.

Term of scheme: Five years.

Minimum investment: Depends on scheme operator.

Maximum investment: £100,000 in any fiscal year.

Tax concessions: * Income tax relief at 20% on subscriptions for shares * No capital gains tax on disposals after five years * Deferral of capital gains tax on previous gains. * If investment is a total loss, further income tax relief at your marginal rate may be claimed on the net cost (after tax relief) of the initial investment.

Restrictions: Investments must be held for the minimum of five years to benefit from tax concessions. * Companies must remain 'qualifying' and 'unquoted'.

Early encashment penalties: * Clawback of initial 20% income tax relief * Loss of capital gains tax exemption * Crystallization of any capital gains tax deferred through making the investment.

Access to cash: Only if the shares can be sold.

Scheme operators: Company promoters.

Charges and costs: Depends on scheme operator: can be up to 8% of the capital raised for the company.

APPENDIX II ‖ *Useful Addresses and Contact Numbers*

Where to Get More Information and Advice

Personal equity plans

> Association of Unit Trusts and Investment Funds
> 65 Kingsway
> London WC2B 6TD
> Tel: 0171 831 0898

Publishes a range of leaflets on unit trusts, also data on the average performance of different types of unit trust.

> Association of Investment Trust Companies
> Park House
> 16 Finsbury Circus
> London EC2M 7JJ
> Tel: 0171 588 5347

Publishes leaflets on investment trusts and produces a monthly performance summary.

> Pepguide
> Chase de Vere Investments Plc
> 63 Lincoln's Inn Fields
> London WC2 3JX
> Tel: 0800 526092

Pepguide, the definitive guide to PEPs, comes in two parts, the first containing details of all currently available plans and the second containing historic performance data.

Performance data on unit and investment trusts may be found in the monthly magazines (available on newsstands):

> *What Investment?*
> 4 Tabernacle Street
> London EC2B 2BH

> *Money Observer*
> 4th Floor
> 75 Farringdon Road,
> London EC1M 3JY

TESSAs

Most banks and building societies have leaflets on their own accounts available at their branches.

Comparative data on the interest rates currently paid on TESSAs may be found in:

> *Moneyfacts*
> Laundry Loke
> North Walsham
> Norfolk NR28 0BD
> Tel: 01692 500765

Personal pensions and AVCs

Detailed information on all available personal pension plans is contained in the annual *Financial Times Personal Pension Handbook*

> *Financial Times Business Information*
> 102 Clerkenwell Road
> London WC1M 5SA
> Tel: 0171 814 9770

Performance data on unit-linked pension funds is contained in the monthly magazines *Money Management* and *Planned Savings* (for addresses see below)

Money Management's annual survey on personal pension plans is published in its October issue. This contains up-to-date information on charges and performance for all available plans.

Free standing additional voluntary contribution plans

Surveys of available plans may be found in:

> *Money Management*
> 3rd Floor
> Maple House
> 149 Tottenham Court Road
> London W1P 9LL
> Tel: 0171 896 2525

> *Planned Savings*
> 33–9 Bowling Green Lane
> London EC1R 0DA
> Tel: 0171 837 1212

Self invested personal pensions

Two of the major providers of these schemes are:

> Winterthur Life
> Provident Way
> Basingstoke
> Hampshire RG21 2SZ
> Tel: 01256 470707

Personal Pensions Management
Rolfes House
60 Milford Street
Salisbury
Wiltshire SP1 2BP
Tel: 01722 414888

Enterprise investment scheme

The principal packager of tax-avoidance schemes under the EIS is:

Johnson Fry
20 Regent Street
London SW1Y 4PZ

Venture capital trusts

Contact the Association of Investment Trust Companies (for address see above) for information on these funds.

Forestry

Consult an independent adviser.

Enterprise zones

Consult an independent adviser.

Tax-exempt friendly societies

Two of the largest societies are:

Family Assurance

Homeowners Friendly Society

Independent financial advice

If you wish to obtain details of IFAs in your local area, contact:

> IFA Promotion Ltd
> 4th Floor
> 28 Greville Street
> London EC1N 8SU
> Tel: 0171 971 1177

They will send you a list of six firms in your area.

The Institute of Financial Planning is a body with membership drawn from accountants and independent financial advisers. Most operate on a fee basis and rebate commissions on any products you buy.

> Institute of Financial Planning
> Whitefriars Centre
> Lewins Mead
> Bristol BS1 2NT
> Tel: 0117 930 4434

Money Management (for address see above) operates a register of independent financial advisers who operate on a fee basis, and will provide a list of such advisers in your area.

APPENDIX III | *Compound Interest Tables*

Tables for Monthly Savings and Lump Sum Investments

Regular Savings

Fund accumulated from regular saving of £100 per month

End of year	Annual rate of return net of charges				
	6%	8%	10%	12%	15%
1	£1,240	£1,250	£1,265	£1,280	£1,295
2	£2,515	£2,605	£2,655	£2,710	£2,785
3	£3,945	£4,060	£4,185	£4,310	£4,500
4	£5,420	£5,640	£5,870	£6,100	£6,485
5	£6,980	£7,340	£7,720	£8,110	£8,735
6	£8,640	£9,180	£9,755	£10,360	£11,340
7	£10,400	£11,170	£11,990	£12,880	£14,340
8	£12,260	£13,310	£14,455	£15,700	£17,780
9	£14,240	£15,630	£17,165	£18,860	£21,745
10	£16,330	£18,130	£20,145	£22,405	£26,300
15	£28,830	£36,930	£41,895	£47,595	£61,640
20	£45,565	£57,270	£72,400	£91,985	£132,710
25	£67,960	£91,485	£124,310	£170,220	£275,655

Capital

Fund accumulated from initial investment of £1,000

End of year	Annual return net of charges				
	6%	8%	10%	12%	15%
1	£1,060	£1,080	£1,100	£1,120	£1,150
2	£1,125	£1,165	£1,210	£1,255	£1,320
3	£1,190	£1,260	£1,330	£1,405	£1,520
4	£1,260	£1,360	£1,465	£1,575	£1,750
5	£1,340	£1,470	£1,610	£1,760	£2,010
6	£1,420	£1,590	£1,770	£1,975	£2,315
7	£1,505	£1,715	£1,950	£2,210	£2,660
8	£1,595	£1,850	£2,145	£2,475	£3,060
9	£1,690	£2,000	£2,360	£2,775	£3,520
10	£1,790	£2,160	£2,595	£3,105	£4,045
15	£2,400	£3,170	£4,180	£5,475	£8,140
20	£3,210	£4,660	£6,730	£9,650	£16,370
25	£4,290	£6,850	£10,850	£17,000	£32,920

APPENDIX IV

Figure 1: Inflation and short-term interest rates

%

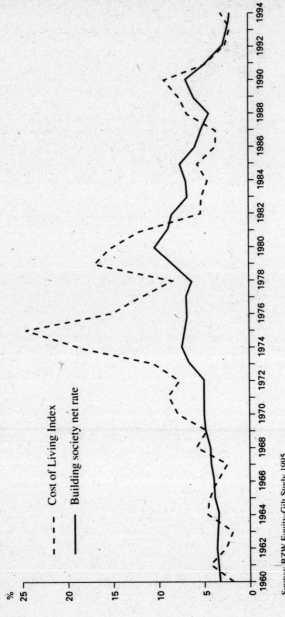

- - - - Cost of Living Index

———— Building society net rate

Source: BZW Equity-Gilt Study 1995

The Cost of Living Index is BZW's index for the UK rate of inflation.
The net rate of interest in a building society account is after deduction of the rate of income tax that
applied in the relevant year, which varied from a high of 41.25% in 1967-70 to a low of 24.4% in 1994.

Figure 2: Fixed interest investments

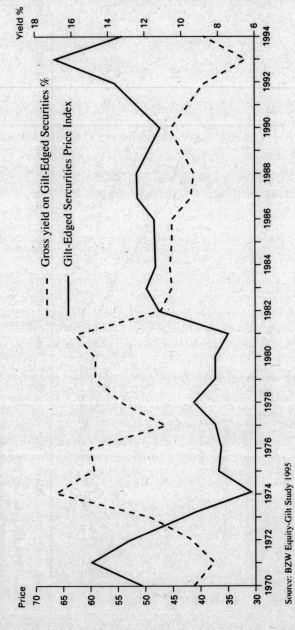

– – – – Gross yield on Gilt-Edged Securities %

———— Gilt-Edged Sercurities Price Index

Source: BZW Equity-Gilt Study 1995

Price and yield figures are for December in each year.

Figure 3: Inflation-adjusted returns from shares, fixed interest and cash deposits

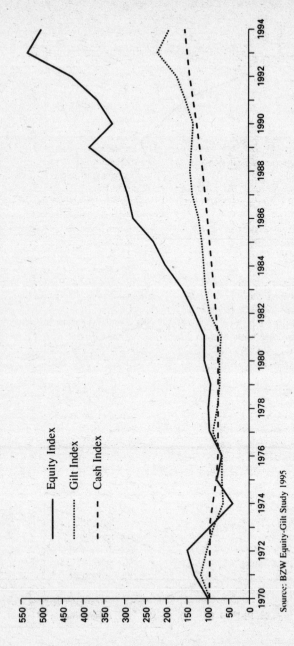

Source: BZW Equity-Gilt Study 1995

The indices are BZW's indices for equities, gilt-edged securities and Treasury Bills calculated at December each year. Gross income is reinvested.

INDEX

The Sunday Times Personal Finance Guide to Your Home

How To Buy, Sell and Pay for It

Diana Wright

Are you thinking of buying a home?

- Should you choose a fixed or variable rate mortgage?
- Should you choose an endowment or Pep mortgage – or a simple repayment?
- How can you save money on insurance?
- How can you get out of negative equity?
- How do you get the best out of an estate agent?
- What is the best mortgage for a second-time buyer?

Your Home – How to Buy, Sell and Pay for It answers these questions and more in simple, jargon-free terms with plenty of clear examples to guide homebuyers – whether first-timers or those buying for the second or third time – through the jungle of competing mortgage, investment and insurance offers.

The book covers all aspects of mortgages – fixed and variable rates, cash-backs and discounts; it weighs up endowment and Pep mortgages, repayments and pension-linked schemes. It provides a simple guide to all insurance matters related to the home, and points the way to saving substantial sums by doing a bit of extra homework.

Buying a home involves the biggest financial decision most people are ever likely to make. This book will help you make the decision which might literally transform the rest of your financial life.

0 00 638704 7

HarperColllinsPaperbacks

The Sunday Times Personal Finance Guide to The Protection Game
A Straightforward Guide to Insurance

Kevin Pratt

Do you have adequate insurance protection and are you getting good value for your premiums?

The Protection Game covers the whole gamut of insurance products, from simple life cover, medical plans and income replacement schemes through to motor and household protection contracts. It is designed to help you build a portfolio of policies that will protect you and your family from the mishaps, misfortunes and tragedies that life so often has to offer.

This guide examines the various insurance policies on the market, describing how they are sold and what they are intended to cover. It cuts through the jargon that often surrounds this area and outlines why and how particular products are appropriate to particular circumstances. *The Protection Game* enables you to:

- remove the mystery and cut through the complexity of insurance
- discover where to get the best value for money
- protect your belongings, your home and your family
- find out what to do when things go wrong

In short, *The Protection Game* addresses everything you need to obtain the priceless gift of peace of mind.

0 00 638702 0

HarperCollinsPaperbacks

The Sunday Times Personal Finance Guide to Your Retirement

How to Plan Wisely for Later Life

Diana Wright

Are you approaching retirement? Do you know:

- How much your pension will be?
- How to trace pensions from previous employers?
- Whether you should take the lump sum from your pension scheme?
- What sort of annuity you should buy and what difference a good choice would make?
- How to rebalance your investment portfolio to suit life after work?
- Where to find good financial advice?
- What sort of insurance you need?

Your Retirement – How to Plan Wisely for Later Life is a practical, informative guide for anyone nearing the end of their working lives. You do not have to be an expert in financial matters to take advantage of the opportunities available. This guide covers an entire range of options including tax planning – how to make the best use of tax-exempt investments, how to avoid the 'age allowance trap' and how to plan for inheritance tax; how to use your home to provide an income; and how some people can improve their pension income by ten per cent or more by making one simple move.

0 00 638707 1

HarperCollinsPaperbacks

Manage Your Time

Sally Garratt

The Successful Manager series
Edited by Bob Garratt

'The working day just isn't long enough . . . I never have enough time'

This, the distress call of so many managers, is something that can be cured. Solving your time management problems will not only make you more efficient day to day, but it will enable you to plan more effectively for your company's future, and spend more time enjoying your personal life.

Sounds impossible? Sally Garratt, who has run numerous personal-effectiveness courses for managers, shows that it can be done. She examines every area of time management – from the telephone and the 'open door', to the diary and setting priorities. She looks at how you cope with meetings, organize your office, the way you plan ahead and how you give work to your staff (if you give work to your staff!) There is an invaluable section on delegation, with advice on when you should and when you shouldn't delegate.

Practical, realistic, and packed with real-life examples, this book will open the door to more effective management of your time.

'It reminds managers of the things they know they should be doing and rarely do. I recommend it for all managers'
Michael Bett, President, Institute of Personnel Management

ISBN 0 00 638411 0

Managing Yourself

Mike Pedler and Tom Boydell

How well do you manage yourself?
Are you in control of your ideas, feelings and actions?
Does your life have purpose and direction?
Have you enough personal energy?

Anyone who wants to improve the way they manage others must first learn to manage themselves. Starting from the inside out, managers need to become more aware of what they are doing in the areas of:

- health – physical, mental and emotional
- skills – social and technical
- action – how you get things done
- identity – valuing and being yourself

This practical guide for the 'thinking manager' contains case studies and useful activities to undertake which are designed to help you increase your effectiveness in managing yourself and your life and in improving your performance both at work and elsewhere.

Published in cooperation with The Association for Management Education and Development.

ISBN 0 00 636892 1

$1000 Billion a Day

Inside the Foreign Exchange Markets

John Roberts

How does the foreign exchange market decide what a currency is worth? What makes exchange rates move unpredictably, often regardless of economic performance? How can foreign exchange dealing amount to many times the value of world trade? Why is London the biggest forex dealing centre – and what does that mean for us?

The value of the pound against other currencies affects how much we pay for everything from cars to coffee. Yet governments and bankers seem unable to control or predict the fluctuations which lead to higher interest rates and reduced public spending, and even experts struggle to explain how the 'market' operates, who manipulates it, how they have acquired such influence, or to whom they are accountable.

John Roberts has talked to company treasurers, delved into bank dealing rooms, and sat alongside brokers at the centre of markets which trade $1,000,000,000,000 a day. Dramatic and revealing, his book exposes the personalities, operations and trends of this crazy world where figures on a screen have the power to bring down governments. It is essential reading for anyone who wants to understand who moves the currency markets, how they do it and why.

ISBN: 0 00 638340 8